WAITING WELL CHANGES
EVERYTHING

A 41-DAY DEVOTIONAL FOR PEOPLE SEEKING AN
ANCHOR IN TIMES OF SHIFTING SAND

KELLY L. MURPHY

Copyright © 2024 by Kelly L. Murphy

All rights reserved.

No part of this book may be reproduced in any form or by any electronic or mechanical means, including information storage and retrieval systems, without written permission from the author, except for the use of brief quotations in a book review.

The Christian Standard Bible. Copyright © 2017 by Holman Bible Publishers. Used by permission. Christian Standard Bible®, and CSB® are federally registered trademarks of Holman Bible Publishers, all rights reserved.

Scripture quotations marked TPT are from The Passion Translation®. Copyright © 2017, 2018, 2020 by Passion & Fire Ministries, Inc. Used by permission. All rights reserved. ThePassionTranslation.com.

Holy Bible, New Living Translation, copyright © 1996, 2004, 2015 by Tyndale House Foundation. Used by permission of Tyndale House Publishers, Inc., Carol Stream, Illinois 60188. All rights reserved.

Taken from the Complete Jewish Bible by David H. Stern. Copyright © 1998. All rights reserved. Used by permission of Messianic Jewish Publishers, 6120 Day Long Lane, Clarksville, MD 21029. www.messianicjewish.net.

Scripture quotations from The Authorized (King James) Version. Rights in the Authorized Version in the United Kingdom are vested in the Crown. Reproduced by permission of the Crown's patentee, Cambridge University Press.

THE HOLY BIBLE, NEW INTERNATIONAL VERSION®, NIV® Copyright © 1973, 1978, 1984, 2011 by Biblica, Inc.® Used by permission. All rights reserved worldwide.

The ESV® Bible (The Holy Bible, English Standard Version®). ESV® Text Edition: 2016. Copyright © 2001 by Crossway, a publishing ministry of Good News Publishers. The ESV® text has been reproduced in cooperation with and by permission of Good News Publishers. Unauthorized reproduction of this publication is prohibited. All rights reserved.

Publisher: LakeView Publications
Cover Design: Bobby Barnhill
Editing: LakeView Publications
Interior Book Formatting: Craig Price & Amanda Price

For bulk ordering information:
Waiting Well Ministries
PO Box 275
Hartland, VT 05048
admin@waitingwell.org

Take me deep, Lord. Out beyond where the waves break. So deep that my toes can't touch the sand to catch my grip. Out where that gentle rocking of the current is like resting in your arms. Deep into the sea, where faith is my only life preserver. Open your truths to me and show me all that you treasure as gold. Overwhelm my life with your presence. I surrender my wants and I pick up your wants for my life, confident that you know the very best in all aspects for me. In Jesus' name I pray.

Amen.

CONTENTS

Acknowledgments   ix
Introduction   xiii

1. Called to a Privileged Position   1
2. A Season of Solitude   9
3. Armor Up!   15
4. What's on Your Cutting Board?   23
5. The Rollercoaster   29
6. A Letter to the Men   35
7. It Seems Like…   41
8. Can You Hear Me Now? How About Now?! Can You Hear Me Now!?   45
9. I Don't Think God Wants Us to Suffer or Be Unhappy   51
10. The Old Prophet: Filtering & Discerning the Advice of Others   57
11. Ask…Seek…Knock…But Don't Get Your Hopes Up   63
12. Is This Your Red Sea Moment? Are You Feeling Like the Israelites?   69
13. So Much Said and Done…   75
14. Why? Why? WHY?!   81
15. Navigating the Exile   89
16. I Was a Water Bug, Skimming Along the Surface of Life's Pond   97
17. Ignoring the Red Flags   103
18. The One Without Sin Casts the First Stone…   109
19. See? See?! If I had Given You What You Wanted…   117
20. The Power of Prayer and Fasting, According to Jesus   121
21. King Jehoshaphat, Paul and Silas   127
22. Resist the Urge to Go Fishing!   135

23. When God Orchestrates a Negative to Gain a Positive...	141
24. When What You've Been Praying for Just Took a Derailment...	147
25. Jonah and His Sailing Companions: Part One	155
26. Jonah and His Sailing Companions: Part Two	161
27. Happy Times Don't Build Endurance and Perseverance	167
28. Dreams, Signs and Reinforcements	173
29. Binding Up and Filling Up	179
30. The Power of Words	185
31. Releasing How We Think it Should All Go	193
32. My Marriage Was Not Blessed by God, so Maybe I'm Not Supposed to be Standing	199
33. What Am I Doing Wrong? I Don't Understand Why It's Taking So Long for God to Move.	205
34. Consequences for "Venting"	211
35. Partial Obedience is Still Disobedience	217
36. For your Children's Children...	225
37. Take Your Eyes Off the Circumstances. Focus on Me	231
38. The Day After Breakthrough	237
39. Back to the Beginning	243
40. Forty Days	249
41. Walking Out of the Wilderness...Lessons Learned of Love and Marriage in a Season of Waiting	255
Stand Anchored on the Promises	265
Scriptures & Notations Day by Day	277
About the Author	285
About the Publisher	287

~ GRATEFUL ~

Only God can take that which broke you into a million pieces and rearrange the rubble, remove the debris within your heart, and make all things new, resulting in this tremendous appreciation for the very implosion that wrecked you. There are truly no adequate sentiments or prayers to show my gratitude for this eight-year journey. I will never stop giving you all the glory, God.

I vividly remember kneeling in prayer and staring at 2 Corinthians 5:18, feeling so utterly insufficient and unqualified for the task God had just placed on my heart: *Now go tell them what I've shown you.* How do I do this? Where do I even begin? God knew, and He provided.

I am so grateful for the many God-orchestrated moments and special people who have shared their pain, experiences, and prayers with me from around the world. Only God could connect me, a woman writing in rural Vermont, USA, with Yvette, a woman on an island in the middle of the Indian Ocean, who needed the very messages God placed on my heart to write and share on social media. When discouragement and questioning set in, God blessed me with so many long-distance connections as beautiful reminders to stay the course.

Special appreciation to my tribes: "The Pea Pod," "Sisterhood of the Traveling Mustard Seed," and the women of Riverbank Church for your support, love, and encouragement.

To Micky Blair (aka My Naomi): Thank you for always grounding our conversations in scripture, for teaching me the importance of staying low and ministering from the overflow, and for always being true to the Holy Spirit's guidance, even when it wasn't what I wanted to hear. I am grateful far beyond what these words could ever express for your presence in my life.

To my Four Life-Changing Blessings, Amanda, Cortni, Keegan and Kate: I could write a book just on your impact in my life and my appreciation for you, but far more valuable is my prayer of 1 Chronicles 4:10 over each of you. To my bonus sons-in-law, Mike, Bryan, and Dan: I thank you for loving and supporting my daughters in ways that always honor and point them to Jesus. To my children's children: Your Meemaw loves you!

And to the one who once asked me, "When we get to Heaven, do you think God will show us how many times He tried?" ... I now know it doesn't matter how many times we fell short, because without that journey, I would have never learned Waiting Well truly does Change Everything.

WAITING WELL CHANGES
EVERYTHING

A 41-DAY DEVOTIONAL FOR PEOPLE SEEKING AN
ANCHOR IN TIMES OF SHIFTING SAND

KELLY L. MURPHY

INTRODUCTION

My marriage was as typical as second marriages go when blending one parent's two kids from a previous marriage into a new relationship. Our courtship began just as my twin daughters entered kindergarten, so as a newlywed couple, we never really knew life outside of ball games, open houses, and sleepovers. When our son and daughter were born into the family, our home blossomed to six humans, two dogs, one cat, a fish and all the time commitments that came with a full nest and two career parents.

The term "date night" was seldom a luxury we found time or energy to coordinate unless our work schedules and social commitments didn't already occupy the week. When the hamster wheel of life started spinning faster, we were so focused on holding everything together, that we never saw the rust and corrosion deteriorating the nuts and bolts of our marriage ... until the bolt broke, and the spinning wheel came to an abrupt stop.

INTRODUCTION

> *Even now–this is the Lord's declaration - turn to me with all your heart, with fasting, weeping and mourning.*
>
> — JOEL 2:12

I'd love to take a fictional route at this point in recounting my story and say I did just that, turning to God in my most devastating time, seeking protection and healing under His wing. But I cannot. In hindsight, I now see how the enemy walked through a wide-open door, because I navigated life with a surface level faith, void of a relationship with God and scripture to anchor and guide me through the storm.

With no acceptable answers that would soothe my pain, my heart was rapidly hardening, and I mentally began walking away. In a startlingly brief amount of time, I convinced myself that it didn't matter if I wasn't enough for my spouse; I would be enough for me. And so I turned inward to myself. I was going to be the hero of my story and the healer of my heart. Prideful arrogance became the plaster cast surrounding all my brokenness, and the opinions of others were signatures and messages written and stamped all over that cast.

During the year that followed the implosion of our relationship, my husband fought hard to keep our marriage intact. And yet, the enemy waged a battle with triggers purposed to blind and distract me. I didn't see a man trying to save his relationship. I believed the whisper that said I was never enough for him while he had me, so why would he fight so hard to keep me? For every effort he gave, I placed another brick on the wall between us. Until he finally surrendered to my fortress.

Make no mistake about this truth ... the enemy is a master at overwhelming us with lies. In what sounds like our own voices, he reaches back into our past with whispered reminders of what we've long since forgotten, working diligently and covertly to ensnare us once again.

He doesn't want me. Trust can never be restored. Nothing will ever change.

My stone wall was piled high with so many of these distorted messages, but it was me turning inward that served as the cement holding the wall in place. It's ironic that the freedom we seek from a painful situation is even equated with "moving on". It's just another deceptive lie to think moving on provides freedom and distance from emotional suffering. We seek fresh starts through other relationships. We look to other humans to fill gaps and voids that they were never designed nor intended to fill. We look at the world and its deceptive ways for distractions. We subconsciously scan the horizon for any sources of new beginnings: a different job, relationship, material purchases, or physically moving away from the place where we were hurt.

After living a divorced life for only seven months, God stirred significantly within my soul. I was beyond baffled. I couldn't understand why and where the internal convictions were coming from, but God knew long ago that the death of my marriage would become the beginning of my heart's alignment under His authority, with my soul forever grafted into His Kingdom.

INTRODUCTION

> *Turn to me and be saved, all the ends of the earth.*
> *For I am God, and there is no other.*
>
> — ISAIAH 45:22

This time, with a humbled and repentant heart, I turned to God. Through a renewed and surrendered life, I learned what anchored faith and waiting well upon His promises really meant. I began writing with immense awe and inspiration, as God's wisdom and discernment guided my words. And I began walking daily in joy, hope, peace, and patience, all described as gifts of the Holy Spirit, but not ones I had experienced before.

At the beginning of compiling this devotional, I cried out to God, "How can I even write this book?! I'm not qualified, not worthy, not restored." It was at this very raw tearful moment that God showed me 2 Corinthians 5:18, and I heard His whisper … First, it's about you and me. I will reconcile your heart with me, and then, together, we will walk in the ministry of reconciliation with others. In His gentle timing, I was shown that the very thing which broke me would be the means through which He would reach and bless others through me.

It is only through my personal walk with Jesus that I can so boldly declare to you, Waiting Well Truly Does Change **Everything**. And it is with an obedient heart and a surrendered pen I obey God's directive of me:

Now go tell them what I've shown you.

INTRODUCTION

In these painful, maybe even hopeless, moments, God has brought us together in this time for His purpose. Know that your courage and strength will come from the Lord, and you can turn the pages each day with confidence that remarkable insights and blessings will result from an open heart, a willingness to receive, and prayerful contemplation.

Praying for you,

Kelly J Murphy

CALLED TO A PRIVILEGED POSITION

DAY 1

Did you know "standers" (those steadfastly waiting for the Lord) are seated and called into a privileged position? Despite the grave situations, despite the latest flareups, dysfunctions and perceived dead ends, and despite every manipulative lie and effort of the enemy to have us believe God's promises are beyond fulfilment, He calls us to stand firm. Sometimes God's plan is not for a modest movement, but a full-on rising from the tomb kind of miracle, just like Lazarus' testimony.

Mary and Martha spent months listening to Jesus' teachings at His feet. They believed in who He was as The Messiah, Son of God, and yet, when Lazarus' death was officially declared, the Bible doesn't record a single person who stood firm and said, "This is not over! Jesus has not arrived yet!"

John clearly stated how Jesus felt:

> *Now Jesus loved Martha, her sister, and Lazarus. So when he heard that Lazarus was sick, he stayed two more days in the place where he was."*
>
> — JOHN 11:5-6

Wait. Did you catch that little two letter word? "So …" John just stated how much Jesus loved them … "So" He delayed His arrival by two more days?! That makes no sense!

I can imagine Mary and Martha kneeling next to Lazarus' bedside in prayer and then taking turns running outside to see if Jesus was about to arrive. Where was He? Didn't He get our message? Doesn't He know how desperate we are? He said He loved us!

It was BECAUSE Jesus loved them that He didn't act immediately when they called upon Him in their time of need. That's a hard truth to accept. When I am fervently seeking God to move in response to my prayer, I am also seeking rapid response, not a delay. And yet, God sees beyond our vantage point to a greater good. He sees ahead of what we understand to be the story in motion.

> *… Our friend Lazarus has fallen asleep, but I'm on my way to wake him up," Jesus told his disciples.*
>
> — JOHN 11:11

Mary and Martha, and those present to support their grieving family, all believed it was too late for a miraculous healing like they'd seen of so many others. After all, Lazarus had been in the tomb for four days when Jesus finally arrived. That's four days of confusion, resentment, and frustration building within Mary and Martha. There were no phones, no mail, no messages, no nothing to calm their nerves and soothe their sorrow. Where was Jesus?! Why didn't He come? It's all over now. He is too late.

It was at this point that I realized God calls us, you and me, to a privileged position as "standers". Do you feel it's too late, or it's all over? Because the divorce papers were signed, sealed, and served. Because there's a canyon of silence and separation in the situation. Because every new door and opportunity becomes a dead end. Because you've prayed and heard nothing.

The rest of the world may declare it's too late. The rest of the world may doubt the ability of God to move in impossible situations. But God has placed us in a privileged position, like Mary and Martha, to watch Him call forth what was once dead into life.

I can imagine myself at Lazarus' tomb, being the one to passionately yell, "It's not over yet! Jesus hasn't arrived! I don't care what it smells like; Jesus is coming!"

It's so important for us to realize that God often delays movement in what we are praying for so that the situation can be declared dead by our standards. He allows the situation to move beyond any revival by our efforts, in our timing, so that only God's glory can be gained.

Truth be told, I like to help God, especially when I don't see Him actively working in the ways or the speed I think He should. But a dead end doesn't mean it's over and done. Sometimes what appears to be a dead end simply means God is the ONLY one who can turn it around, breathe life back into it, and gain the glory. Our role is to STAND in faith and WAIT through trust.

Upon receiving the message of Lazarus' illness, *Jesus said,*

> *This sickness will not end in death but is for the glory of God, so that the Son of God may be glorified through it.*
>
> — JOHN 11:4

He gave the disciples the end of the story, but they missed the significance of His foretelling. It certainly wasn't missed by me! Several years ago, the Holy Spirit spoke through a prophetic friend and said to me, "Kelly, God is saying, 'I've given you the end of the story. Are you going to trust me with how we get there?'"

Well, didn't THAT just cause me to pause!! God gave Sarah and Abraham the end of their story about birthing nations, but they had to trust Him within a very long season of waiting. David was identified and chosen as king, but first had to trust God through all the trials before he would wear the crown. Jesus foretold the end of Lazarus' story, but friends and family had not yet learned to trust HIM more than what their eyes could only see in the natural.

God calls us to stand because He intends to move within the situation, albeit not in our timing or our preferred ways. As we walk out these upcoming days together, I urge you to step into owning your privileged position for what it is. We're sitting in the greatest front-row seat, to watch the power of God on display, as He moves mightily within our situations.

The Lord does not delay his promise, as some understand delay, but is patient with you, not wanting any to perish but all to come to repentance.

— 2 PETER 3:9

REFLECTION QUESTIONS:

1. What in my life do I consider dead, impossible to resurrect or change, and am I waiting in anticipation for Jesus to answer those prayers?
2. In what ways have I already seen the Lord work because of my privileged position, and have I offered praise and gratitude for those ways?
3. In moments of despair, who do I relate to more: the person stating Jesus has arrived too late, or the person in the crowd who declares, "it's not too late! Jesus is coming! Have faith!"

PRAYER PAUSE:

Lord, this position I am in, this situation swirling around me, is not a surprise to you. While the position doesn't feel like a privilege, I ask that you begin unpacking what I am to learn within it and how you want to transform me through it. While my eyes may see death in the details, my heart will declare, "It's not too late ... Jesus is here! I will have faith." Holy Spirit, please open your truths to me. Show me how to pray bold prayers in moments of weakness. It's in Jesus' name, I pray. Amen.

KELLY L. MURPHY

WAITING WELL CHANGES EVERYTHING

A SEASON OF SOLITUDE

DAY 2

Standing on a promise from God can feel incredibly lonely. But did you know God often orchestrates wilderness seasons of quiet, solitude, and isolation so that we can learn to hear and distinguish His voice from all the other voices that bombard our lives? I know this all too well.

I obediently followed God's every request to abide, but there came a time when the silence was utterly painful to my ears. Why, God? This walk is so very hard! Why would you orchestrate isolation from others?

"Because it's in the quiet and the wilderness that you learn to hear MY voice. Have you noticed there is no noise, chaos or competing attention in MY solitude? It's just you and me."

Whoa ... This was the very first time I heard the voice of the Holy Spirit so clearly and distinctly. Discernment from the Lord washed over me in the moments that followed. If I don't learn to distinguish the voice of God now in this season of waiting, how will I ever be able to distinguish God's voice when that promise is fulfilled? How will I recognize God's voice from triggers and influences of the enemy?

Truth be told, I fell prey to the enemy in more ways than you have time to read. I took the bait when the enemy used other people to trigger old wounds within me. I had no way of discerning the voice of the Holy Spirit from the voice of my independent, self-determined lifestyle. I filled my life with family, community, and work commitments, but had no margin to hear God's voice or seek His direction. I intentionally made my life so busy to avoid the quiet.

That was until I surrendered to this God-orchestrated season of separation, and in doing so, allowed it to become my spiritual boot camp, learning obedience and how to distinguish the sound of my heavenly Father's voice from all the worldly traffic and chaos. If I couldn't accurately recognize His voice, how could I ever accurately answer His call in this period of learning to wait well?

I started placing space, time, and margin in my life by honoring God's directive of physical rest. I worked six days and purposefully gave the seventh to Him. (Watch how the enemy organizes all kinds of social commitments when you commit and dedicate to a day of rest!) But I learned to say no! I began praying for wisdom and discernment from the Holy Spirit before I opened the pages of God's Word. And I became comfortable talking with God all the time. Seriously, ALL. THE. TIME! In the car. Doing chores. Sitting in traffic. Cooking supper. Taking a shower. My prayer time transformed from a dedicated moment in the morning or night to literally a conversation lasting the entire day. I talked, and God listened. And when He talked, whoa, I could now hear Him deep within my soul! I became hungry to hear more.

Friends, what may start out as a very uncomfortable season of solitude will most assuredly transform into a beautifully purposed and orchestrated communication with God, because it is His heart and very nature to draw us near.

> *Come to me, all you who are weary and burdened, and I will give you rest. Take my yoke upon you and learn from me, for I am gentle and humble in heart, and you will find rest for your souls. For my yoke is easy and my burden is light.*
>
> *— MATTHEW 11:28-30*

> *You were shown these things so that you would know that the Lord is God; there is no other besides Him. He let you hear his voice from heaven to instruct you.*
>
> *— DEUTERONOMY 4:36*

> *Now, if any of you lacks wisdom, he should ask God–who gives to all generously and ungrudgingly–and it will be given to him. But let him ask in faith without doubting.*
>
> *— JAMES 1:5-6*

REFLECTION QUESTIONS:

1. What is one immediate change you can make in your life to hear God more clearly? What is one immediate change you can make to your schedule to experience God more deeply?
2. Do words like abide, be still and seek solitude make you uncomfortable? Is your life filled with background noise to avoid the quiet?
3. Each day for the next week, set a timer for five minutes. Ask God to enter those five minutes and sit in silence. No reading, no making to-do lists. Just silence and stillness, seeking to hear his voice. Next week, add five minutes to the time. At the start of the third week, add another five minutes, and so on. Remember, it's not about the total quantity of minutes you devote but rather the quality of those moments connected to our Heavenly Father with an open, receiving heart.

_____

_____

_____

_____

_____

_____

_____

WAITING WELL CHANGES EVERYTHING

ARMOR UP!

DAY 3

"I don't know how to stop the thoughts in my mind."

"I feel like I'm circling the drain of negativity, and I can't stop it."

Sound familiar? Those thoughts, and so many more, can be a constant barrage of messages overwhelming our minds when standing on a promise from God. We can be unsuspecting pawns in the hands of an enemy that remembers every little painful trigger better than we do and he never fails to use them all against us.

To not only survive this season, but thrive within the journey, I need to stop the poisonous adrenaline streaming through my body, activated from the painful messages on repeat in my mind. I need skillful, perfectly chosen tools to deflect those fiery darts lodged by the enemy into my soul. With the Bible as my only trusted source of guidance, I search for the nuggets of wisdom to help me move beyond the destructive mental loops. Each word of scripture becomes like Neosporin applied to the burns and abrasions on my soul. I open to Ephesians 6 and start discovering and studying a supernatural collection of tools only God could inspire.

When Paul wrote his letter to the people living in Ephesus, also called the book of Ephesians, the average citizen was familiar with Roman soldiers walking in their clanking metal armor and seeing their intimidating presence everywhere. When the Holy Spirit inspired Paul to write the correlation between this armor and the very real spiritual battle of every believer, it was a picture anyone could understand, regardless of their status within society.

Today, a person standing on a promise from God faces the same fiery spiritual arrows through interactions with family, friends, co-workers, and even our Christian influences, all purposed by the enemy to infiltrate our peace, joy, and contentment. In my own recent moments of struggle, God gave me a new perspective on this old armor, prompting me to pray as if it were literal, physical items to put on:

Hiking Boots of PEACE ... Slide your feet into waterproof, steel-toed hiking boots of God's peace and direction, as you climb up the steep, rocky terrain in mountain situations and across rivers and valleys of uncertainty, filled with muck, mud, and mire. Feel the straps and laces tethered and tied securely around your ankles for stability and the comfort of cushioned insoles and structured leather for balance in any challenging situation.

> *Abundant peace belongs to those who love your instruction; nothing makes them stumble.*
>
> — PSALMS 119 CSB

Safety Harness of TRUTH ... Jesus said,

> *You will know the truth, and the truth will set you free.*
>
> — JOHN 8:32

Secure the ever-present truth of who God is around your waist, as if it were a wide, buckled safety harness, stabilizing your spine during all your days, not just for those times of heavy lifting.

Bullet-Proof Vest of RIGHTEOUSNESS... Imagine God has given you a fire and bullet-proof vest, to wrap around your core, protecting your heart, lungs, and all other vital life-giving organs. This vest is the protection that manifests from right standing with the Lord, deflecting and diffusing ammunition and triggers covertly lodged by an enemy we cannot see but one who remembers our weakest moments.

> *For the Lord becomes your personal bodyguard as you follow his ways, protecting and guarding you as you choose what is right.*
>
> — PROVERBS 2:7 TPT

Motorcycle Helmet of SALVATION ... Allow God's salvation to become like a full-face defensive motorcycle helmet, protecting your mind and eyes from the lies and manipulations of the enemy. The firmly padded chin guard securely protects your tongue and mouth, guarding words for greater intentionality and less damage.

This impermeable helmet means distractions and messages purposed to move your focus to everything, but God are deflected and denied access into your mind. Jesus *said,*

> *I tell you the truth, those who listen to my message and believe in God who sent me have eternal life. They will never be condemned for their sins, but they have already passed from death into life.*
>
> — JOHN 5:24 NLT

With your body now geared up and protected, reach out and grasp the massive Shield of FAITHFULNESS in your left hand. At one time I believed this shield to be my own faithfulness in God, acting as the protectant. But my faith can often resemble a torn and battered piece of aluminum foil used during a barbeque, hardly exuding strength and durability! Then I read Psalms 91:4 and this shield suddenly made sense:

> *He will cover you with his feathers; you will take refuge under his wings. HIS FAITHFULNESS WILL BE A PROTECTIVE SHIELD.*
>
> — PSALMS 91:4

God's faithfulness to me is the shield!! Now that's some serious strength and durability, acting as a barrier from your boots to your helmet, light enough to carry on long journeys and through treacherous seasons, but thick and heavy enough to protect you from all those fiery darts.

And last, in your right hand, pick up the double-edged light saber of His WORD. Imagine the sounds of that Star Wars-like saber, slicing through all the world holds as its "truth," with its never dull, always sharpened blade of brilliant light. It's the only offensive weapon needed in your full body defense against a spiritual battle that rages every hour of every day when standing on a promise from God.

> *For the word of God is living and effective and sharper than any double-edged sword, penetrating as far as the separation of soul and spirit, joints, and marrow. It is able to judge the thoughts and intentions of the heart.*
>
> — HEBREWS 4:12

When those negative thoughts swirl in my mind, whispering things will never change, whispering that person will never see differently, whispering I'm not good enough or that situation is impossible, telling me I should give up and move on ... you know all those fiery darts ... I stop and pray on the motorcycle helmet, and the sucking sound from circling the proverbial drain immediately stops. When my heart physically hurts and I find it hard to breathe from the latest disappointment, I put on the bulletproof vest of righteousness and belt of God's truth. And when my feet are sore and blistered from long suffering and enduring this walk, it's the hiking boots of peace that renew and rejuvenate my stride.

Using armor in spiritual warfare wasn't just a message Paul was writing to the Ephesians. It was a message of hope he was delivering, while often residing in his own physical and literal prison. We stand defiant against an enemy that lost the battle when Jesus died and was resurrected three days later. We also stand in the gap of faith for our loved ones, fully armored and confident that God will fight this battle for us.

> *Finally, be strengthened by the Lord and by his vast strength. Put on the full armor of God so that you can stand against the schemes of the devil. For our struggle is not against flesh and blood, but against the rulers, against the authorities, against the cosmic powers of this darkness, against evil spiritual forces in the heavens. For this reason, take up the full armor of God, so that you may be able to resist in the evil day, and having prepared everything, to take your stand.*
>
> — EPHESIANS 6:10-13

REFLECTION QUESTION:

Before your feet hit the floor and you stand to take on a new day, physically imagine putting on each piece of armor through prayer. Do you notice a difference?

PRAYER PAUSE:

"Lord, today I choose to put on the hiking boots of peace. Let your unwavering peace be the foundation upon which I walk. Guide me with steady steps through uncertain valleys and over rocky terrain.

May your peace be the source of my stability, cushioning my every step and allowing me to navigate any difficult situation. Wrap me in the safety harness of truth. Let your eternal truth be the belt that secures and strengthens me. May it be the constant reminder of who you are to me and of who I am to you. Let this knowledge direct my every action.

Today, I choose the bullet-proof vest of righteousness. May this knowledge of your completed work on the cross deflect the hidden attacks and negativity that threaten my spirit.

Today, I slide on the motorcycle helmet of salvation. Let this shield guard my thoughts and vision from the lies, distractions, and manipulations of the enemy. I am your child. Redeemed, loved, wanted, and treasured. Nothing I could ever do would take your cleansing power away from me.

Today, I choose to pick up the shield of faithfulness. It is not my own faith that offers true protection, but yours. Let your unwavering faithfulness be the impenetrable barrier that surrounds me, reaching from the ground to the crown of my head.

Today, I choose the double-edged lightsaber of your Word. May its unwavering truth, powerful and ever-present, cut through the world's distortions. Let it be the only weapon I need in this ongoing spiritual battle, allowing me to stand firm on your promises.

Thank you for your unfailing protection, Lord. In your name I pray, Amen.

_____

_____

WHAT'S ON YOUR CUTTING BOARD?

DAY 4

Have you ever taken a raw chicken breast, one of those thick ones that are bigger than your hand, and just tried to tear it apart? It's ridiculously hard to do without using a knife. The fibers are so tightly joined you can't just rip them apart. Marriage is no different.

Truthfully, I never understood the magnitude of divorce and why God hates it until after I had cut it in two. Sometimes you don't even know how you got there, but one day you're standing at the kitchen counter, with a knife in hand, and the raw chicken breast laying exposed on that cutting board. Even if your marriage appears dead and you feel it is time to cut your losses, I urge you to pause, put the knife down and step away from the counter.

What you don't know and can't comprehend at this moment is that the relief you seek is not to be found by cutting and separating. There will be an ache so deep within you, a void you will always feel, and a sense of disappointment so profound. Yes, you can bury it with another relationship, material possessions, work, alcohol, drugs, and hobbies, but those are all diversions and distractions from the truth that a living thing was created when you were married, that binds and weaves together your children, memories, struggles and achievements. Everyday moments with your spouse create fibrous strands in your marriage, giving it strength and endurance.

> *There was a reason Jesus said, "So they are no longer two, but one flesh. Therefore, what God has joined together, let no one separate."*
>
> — MATTHEW 19:6

Grasping the knife gives you control of the situation and temporary relief, but that control is at the expense of allowing God to heal, allowing God to truly do what He does best, which is to take what you deem as impossible and transform it into something that magnifies and testifies to just how glorious he is.

Don't get me wrong, I understand the enticement of holding the knife in your hand to do the cutting. You think it can't get any worse or feel any more painful than in that moment. But it can and it actually will. What I've learned through divorce is that there is truly nothing God can't fix. Nothing is impossible for Him. God despises divorce because He knows that, once you cut it with a knife, it's harder to heal your wounds, and those scars will last your lifetime.

It took two broken marriages for me to realize the profound sanctity of marriage. God's Spirit, His love, and His commitment are invisibly woven within those fibers. Yes, even when you feel like it's dead and beyond hope. He knows what you're currently going through. He knows what your life will be like after you cut the marriage in two.

Surrender the knife to Him and allow the Word of God to...

> *...cut right through to where soul meets spirit and joints meet marrow, [because the Word is] quick to judge the inner reflections and attitudes of the heart.*
>
> — HEBREWS 4:12 CJB

Ask the Holy Spirit to expose the lies and deceptions of the enemy. Request wisdom and discernment to act as a filter in all decisions and conversations. Allow God to reveal and transform, reconcile, and restore.

If you are walking through a situation that seems impossible, I ask you to put down the knife of action on that decision while you read this devotional. Pause. Back away from the cutting board. Passionately seek the Lord through each day of this devotional, as if it is your God-ordained miracle in the waiting.

> *The Lord is near to all who call upon Him, to all who call upon Him in truth.*
>
> — PSALMS 145:18 CSB

REFLECTION QUESTIONS:

1. What are those memories and experiences within your relationship that have acted as fibrous strands binding you together?
2. When you read "nothing is impossible for God," what is your honest reaction? Doubt? Skepticism? Disbelief?

PRAYER PAUSE:

I am putting down the knife, Lord. I am backing away from the cutting board in an act of surrendering the situation to you. Please calm this urgency within me to move beyond the pain. Begin a transformation within me, becoming the person you designed me to be. Show me how to forgive, how to extend the same grace and mercy that you have given me. Jesus, your word says NOTHING is impossible for those who believe in you. I ask you to help my disbelief. Heal my own soul wounds that are at the root of the words I speak and the reactions that have become second nature to me. Change is possible, but it must start with me. Show me how to lean into your strength and to rely upon your provision. Open up your truths to me as I walk in a deeper relationship with you. I pray this in your name, Jesus. Amen.

_____

_____

_____

_____

_____

WAITING WELL CHANGES EVERYTHING

THE ROLLERCOASTER

DAY 5

It's a ride every person standing on a promise from God finds themselves initially strapped into, but hardly a ride of amusement to be enjoyed. The enemy smugly stands at the controls, as your raw emotions react to the twists, turns, highs and lows of a ride that never seems to stop. Up and down. Hour by hour. Day after day.

In the early morning, after quiet time with God, I rode a mountaintop view of life. At noontime I was in tears and feeling defeated. Suppertime, I was back to experiencing the ride of the Holy Spirit's power. Only to climb into bed at night, feeling alone, defeated once again, and crying into my pillow. I was a pawn in the hands of an enemy that remembered every little painful trigger better than I did, with pinpoint accuracy, and he never failed to use them all against me.

One of the fruits of the Holy Spirit is self-control, and that was hardly anything you would have seen in me. I was spewing raw emotions to everyone about everything. I'd retell interactions over and over, which continually fueled those emotions. I was desperate for opinions, especially if they agreed with my headspace at that moment.

Then one day the rollercoaster ride reached a permanent standstill. I closed my eyes, imagining myself physically stepping up and out, climbing over and off, placing my feet on hard, unmovable, unshakable holy ground. On that day, I loudly declared the ride was over, in Jesus' name. I asserted, in Jesus' name, that the enemy will not operate the controls over my life anymore. I surrendered everything to God; I mean absolutely everything in my life. Kids, relationships, work, finances, living space, health, career goals, past, present, future ... everything! Then I let go of my plans and dreams, declaring "I'm all in" for whatever God had for my life.

I stood at the ocean on that day of surrender and prayed: "Take me deep, Lord. Out beyond where the waves break. So deep that my toes can't touch the sand to catch my grip. Out where that gentle rocking of the current is like resting in your arms. Deep into the sea, where faith is my only life preserver. Open your truths to me and show me all that you treasure as gold. Overwhelm my life with your presence. I surrender my wants and I pick up your wants for my life, confident that you know the very best in all aspects of me. In Jesus' name I pray. Amen."

The more I surrendered to God and chose His will over my own, the more those emotional highs and lows evened out. The mountain top vistas and lows as deep as my septic system became farther and farther apart. The spikes and valleys resembled an EKG where I ended up flatlining, which I now see as a good thing. In the world, a heartbeat that flat lines means death, but in God's Kingdom, flatlining only means dead to self. We become alive in Him!! No more rollercoaster, no more raw emotions.

If you can relate to the rollercoaster ride, I urge you to keep moving forward. This is a process. Do NOT let the enemy hijack your journey by convincing you that things will never change, or you're failing, or you deserve better, or you're too far gone for God's blessings. All those messages are meant to keep you from discovering this amazing walk with the Lord. The enemy knows that once you get a taste of this authentic experience, his gig is up. No one who climbed off that emotional rollercoaster has ever said, "Oh yes, let me ride it again!" The enemy's amusement ride will be over.

God knows your current situation is a very short segment of time on earth compared to eternity. He is FAR more interested in the alignment of your heart and your posture under His authority for ALL of eternity. In this waiting, there's serious transformation to be done in you. The acceptance of this will move mountains. I know because it has for me!

Close your eyes and physically picture yourself stepping up and out, climbing over and off the rollercoaster to plant your feet on hard, unmovable, unshakable holy ground.

> *I am at rest in God alone; my salvation comes from Him. He alone is my rock and my salvation, my stronghold; I will never be shaken.*
>
> — PSALMS 62:1-2

REFLECTION QUESTIONS:

1. What has the rollercoaster ride felt like for you? What does your climb off the rollercoaster look like?
2. What does your prayer of surrender sound like?
3. What was the last area of your life that you surrendered to God, and what was the result?

_____
_____
_____
_____
_____
_____
_____
_____
_____
_____
_____
_____
_____
_____

A LETTER TO THE MEN

DAY 6

Eleven years ago, my marriage of 12 years imploded. The details of why are irrelevant at this point, but what does matter is that when God tells you to stand and wait for her, it is because HE KNOWS WHY you should wait. God has a plan and purpose that you cannot see in these moments, even in the chaos and dysfunction, even through her hurtful words and actions.

My husband fought hard for our marriage until a few months before the divorce was final. At that point, he listened to the words of those around him when they said to move on. He listened to me, convincing him to move on, declaring that change wasn't possible and trust could not return. Those people and myself did not know that God was going to do a mighty restoration of my unforgiving prodigal heart. They didn't know that God was going to put a new love for him and our marriage into my hardened heart. Neither did I. They just wanted him to stop being sad and find happiness again.

Husbands and Ex-Husbands ... I am urging you to stand firm on what God has called you to do. I know what the softening of the heart feels like. I know what those early days are like when God plants new seeds in your heart. I fought it with every ounce of my being because I just didn't want to admit I made a wrong decision. I didn't think the marriage, him or I could ever be different. It was pride, all pride.

When God calls you to stand, He intends to see you through to reconciliation. Don't give up. I know it's probably the toughest hill you've ever climbed. I know it seems like a dead end and you think she doesn't care anymore. I know her words are cruel. Trust me, I know. I was that wife.

At the same time God was working on the transformation of my heart, the enemy introduced my husband to someone. He called their relationship "easy". He struggled, trying to navigate a relationship with her while being undeniably drawn to God calling Him to our kids, me, and our family. He has navigated years of avoiding God's promptings to step forward in that obedience, as it was in constant opposition to the enemy's enticement of a new life, an easy situation, and a chance to pack away old memories. This journey has been an incredible witnessing to what efforts the enemy will orchestrate to impede the movements of God.

Eight years ago, I made a commitment to God by standing firm in prayer. We've had so many prompts from God. While the enemy has waged a mighty battle through it all, God has continually reaffirmed in me that I am to hold my stance. Don't move. Do not give up despite the lack of positive movement.

WAITING WELL CHANGES EVERYTHING

Men, if you open yourselves up for someone to distract you from the pain, to walk you out of the exile you feel, make no mistake, you'll find a do-all-the-right-things, say-all-the-right-things package. But it won't be a heavenly-orchestrated escort. You'll wake up one day to find a greater prison than you had in the mess of an imploded marriage. The enemy loves to introduce an "easy" relationship with no accountability to be the man God designed you to be. Don't allow your social circle, your family, friends, or co-workers to have more influence in your decisions than what God has said directly to you.

Stand for your marriages—even if you're newly separated, near divorce or beyond divorce. Use this time to chase hard for God, to become the husbands that God has designed you to be. Resist being a "perfect" mate, by placing greater value on the ever-changing words of your wife, as she tells you what she thinks she "needs" in a marriage or a husband. What we "think" we want when separated from God is NOT the same as when our hearts are aligned under God. Don't wander from who God calls you to be in order to be something else to her. Use this time to draw close to God so that when she does return and restoration happens, you're going to be ready for the marriage HE has intended.

Imagine praying with her, reading the Bible with her. Be ready to witness how God has become the superglue in your restored marriage. Please men, don't stop standing, don't stop praying, and most of all, don't stop loving the new woman God is calling and transforming her to be ... in His perfect time. Waiting Well will change everything.

If you do not stand firm in your faith, then you will not stand at all.

— ISAIAH 7:9

WAITING WELL CHANGES EVERYTHING

IT SEEMS LIKE...

DAY 7

... they don't care.

... they're living their best life.

... that change will never happen.

... this promise will never come.

Anytime we use the words "it seems" to describe what we see in the natural realm, it's a safe bet that a forest fire of human analysis is being fueled by our emotions. I think the enemy festers and thrives in the realm of "it seems". When he whispers a message of what something "seems like" into our thought process, disguised as our own voice, it can send us spinning with scenarios of what is "really" going on, how we should act on those scenarios, and what the outcomes should be or will be.

The enemy uses people, circumstances, memories, etc. to trigger us into acting, judging, and condemning, all because of what it appears to be on the surface. We strategize and analyze. To God's chosen people, it "seemed like" life was over when they were literally backed up against the Red Sea. To Sarah, it "seemed like" God's promise of childbirth was laughable at her age.

To Mary and Martha, it "seemed like" the death and burial of Lazarus meant it was over and done.

After reading all these Bible stories, we should know God doesn't operate the way the world would expect. Less is more. The poor are rich. Why would it be any different when we look at our situations? Things are NEVER as they seem. True confession time. I have a perfect track record of being 100% wrong in my judgements and assumptions of what something "seems like". So much so that I hate to even utter the words anymore. I am now learning and striving to seek God for His wisdom and discernment on how I should see a situation before I begin circling the emotional drain. And, if He chooses to not provide me with understanding, then I know I am not meant to receive the information at the time I desire it. But understanding will come when God deems me ready to receive it.

I find it interesting that God knew our inclination to judge a situation by only what we see on the surface. It's the same reason God spoke through Zechariah:

> *The Lord of Armies says this: 'Though it may seem impossible to the remnant of this people in those days, should it also seem impossible to me?'-this is the declaration of the Lord of Armies.*
>
> — ZECHARIAH 8:6

REFLECTION QUESTIONS:

1. What situations have you judged "it seems like"?
2. Have you had a situation that turned out to be something other than what "it seemed like" at the time? How did that impact you?
3. What Bible stories have you read that speak to the judgement of what something seems like in the natural realm?

PRAYER PAUSE:

Lord, in this moment, I give you all my "seems like" judgements. I release my opinions about the people and situations in my life. I know the enemy resides in the surface level details while you seek deeper transformation of the heart. Like Solomon, I seek your wisdom and discernment to be my life's barometer for how things really are. Holy Spirit, convict me immediately when my mind begins to entertain the distractions and lies of the enemy. Place God-honoring people and scripture in front of me to support my daily walk. God, you are the only one who is able to distinguish what is truth from what is false. I give you all the honor and glory rightfully due to you, Amen.

_____

_____

_____

_____

CAN YOU HEAR ME NOW? HOW ABOUT NOW?! CAN YOU HEAR ME NOW!?

DAY 8

We repeat these words in frustration when we don't have consistent cell service during a phone conversation. We will physically move around in a frenzy to create a stronger signal with the remote cell tower. We know that the more directly aligned we are to the tower, the stronger the signal and stronger is our ability to hear and communicate. Imagine if we channeled that urgency into our faith life. Imagine if we aligned our lives with God's signal to remove those moments of garbled communication.

What if God is the one saying to you, "Can you hear me now?"

Is your life so full of distractions and barriers that His Spirit, His signal, can't make it through all that you've allowed into your life? God wants to do life with us all the time—not just in this season of waiting, not just when we want an answer or seek something from Him. He wants us to invite Him into a continual dialogue throughout our day. But He will not go where He is not welcome.

Prayers matter in God's Kingdom, and praying is a communication with Jesus that saturates to the very cellular level of our bodies. So how do we pray bold, effective prayers that strengthen our line of communication with Him? We infuse the very promises of God, the words of His scriptures, into our prayers. When we "pull down" the heavenly promises of God and incorporate them in our prayers, we align ourselves with His will. And God moves.

What does it mean to pull down God's promises? Imagine you walk into a room and there are helium-filled white balloons tied with red ribbons floating above your head. On each balloon is written a promise from God in gold-colored permanent marker.

Just before walking into this room, your heart was shattered by a situation out of your control. With tears rolling down your cheeks, you look up and grab a ribbon in each hand. Pulling down the balloons to your eye level, you read on one,

> *The Lord is near the brokenhearted; he saves those crushed in spirit.*
>
> — PSALMS 34:18

and on the other balloon is written,

> *He heals the brokenhearted and bandages their wounds.*
>
> — PSALMS 147:3

You have just "pulled down," the promises of God. You incorporate those promises in your prayers, "Lord ... your promises are my firm foundation. My broken heart needs you. I'm trusting in your Word and holding your promises in both of my hands, promises that declare you will be near my broken heart, you will bandage my wounds, and you will heal my broken heart ..."

You've just electrified and power-packed your prayers by infusing them with God's own words! Those balloons have been a HUGE game changer in my prayers and faith walk. Every time, and I do mean EVERY time, I grasp a promise of God and include God's specific scripture verses in my prayers, movement happens. Why? Because I am anchoring my conversations directly on His promises. I am placing full faith and trust in the God who NEVER lies to me, and always stays true to His word. But I can't infuse my prayers with promises if I don't know what they are! I urge you to discover the vast treasure of promises guaranteed to strengthen your signal to Him.

> *The name of the Lord is a strong tower; the righteous run to it and are protected.*
>
> — PROVERBS 18:10

REFLECTION QUESTIONS:

1. What scripture verses would you write on balloons?
2. Do you have a prayer on repeat in your mind? Something you continually pray the same way every day? How could

you infuse God's own Words to transform it into a bold request?
3. Write out: *"but those who wait for the Lord shall renew their strength; they shall mount up with wings like eagles; they shall run and not be weary; they shall walk and not faint."* (Isaiah 40:31) and place it on your mirror or somewhere you will see it often each day.

_____
_____
_____
_____
_____
_____
_____
_____
_____
_____
_____
_____
_____
_____
_____
_____

WAITING WELL CHANGES EVERYTHING

I DON'T THINK GOD WANTS US TO SUFFER OR BE UNHAPPY

DAY 9

So, God wouldn't want you to walk through a painful learning season to gain a new freedom you have never experienced before? God wouldn't want you to walk through the fire so that a new you can rise from the ashes? God wouldn't want you to lay your dead or dying marriage on His altar so that He can transform it into your best blessing?

Where do we get this inflated sense of self that says we "deserve" more? Why do we think that a loving God would not allow us to walk through a season of pain? Only the enemy whispers how much more we deserve, are entitled to, and how much we are missing out in life. Of course, God allows pain and suffering. If God orchestrated the importance of His own son's crucifixion, then it's a safe bet He will allow us to go through temporary seasons of pain for a purpose as well.

Honestly, I spent far too much time focused on the circumstances and people around me and far too little time focused on my behaviors, my past mistakes, my own contributions, and accountability to a failed marriage. Do not be deceived. This attitude has roots deeply planted by the enemy. Satan knows power and strength rise from the transformational ashes under God's reign, and he will play unfairly with you to keep you from changing.

The enemy wants you to question God's goodness. The enemy reminds you of your past, causing triggers to continually pull you back into dark places. The enemy twists righteousness into idolatry. Every day, we have a choice of who and what we will follow. What's your choice going to be?

Through tears and anguish, we can shake our fists at God and repeatedly demand an answer to "Why?!?" We can cast blame onto circumstances and people for making us collateral damage to their actions. We can pridefully and independently make decisions, thinking we know best, all meant to fix our own hurting hearts. Or through faith, we can choose to lean in, abide in, and be transformed by God.

Truth is God has allowed this season in our lives. That is a very hard sting of reality to anyone who thinks God should be a cosmic spiritual vending machine of warm, happy times. But giving a child everything they want, every time they want it, does not benefit the child. We place guardrails for safety around our children's playtime and speak boundaries of "no" ahead of their choices, but sometimes they do it, anyway. As they grow and mature, we step back and allow them to make their own mistakes and face the consequences, knowing that we are right beside them to support and nurture endurance and character within them. We unconditionally love them through all the peaks and valleys of life.

God does the same thing with us. He is our perfect parental example of mothering and fathering. He allows pain and suffering into our lives as opportunities for us to be transformed into the likeness of Jesus, with an end goal of eternity, not just this short earthly walk. THIS season, THIS journey that you are on has far more to do with your own relationship with God. He wants this truth deeply planted in your heart.

Don't miss out on the tremendous holy transformation God has planned for you, by focusing more on the details you see with your eyes than what on God will show you within your heart.

> *We can rejoice, too, when we run into problems and trials, for we know that they help us develop endurance. And endurance develops strength of character, and character strengthens our confident hope of salvation. And this hope will not lead to disappointment. For we know how dearly God loves us, because he has given us the Holy Spirit to fill our hearts with his love.*
>
> — ROMANS 5:3-5 NLT

REFLECTION QUESTIONS:

1. Are there ways you may have been treating God like a cosmic vending machine? Praying to receive, disappointed and distanced when what you prayed isn't delivered in your timing?

2. As you reflect on prior prayers, are there opportunities to thank God for not answering the prayers you sought at that time? Can you see His loving hands protecting you at that moment?
3. What is the most recent prayer that God has answered for you?

PRAYER PAUSE:

For the last week, I've provided samples of prayers to build a prayer life of gratitude, reflection, and boldness. Take a step forward in your faith and imagine God is sitting across from you and talk with Him. Confess those times when you may have looked upon God as more of a genie, called upon to grant wishes in line with your plan. Consider those times when God protected you from your prayers and thank Him for each one. Ask Him to show you the details or the impact that you could not see at the time. Ask and be open to receive His insights, not just in that moment, but in the days to come. Give glory and praise for all the prayers God has answered. And then share the burdens upon your heart. Eloquence and choosing the right religious words aren't keys to unlocking answered prayers. God is seeking your surrendered, obedient seeking heart. When all you can muster is "God, my heart is broken. I don't even know what to say," Jesus knows your burdens and hurts. He will intercede and lift your needs to His Father. Sometimes the most powerful words spoken will simply be "Your will be done, God. Not mine."

_____

_____

THE OLD PROPHET: FILTERING & DISCERNING THE ADVICE OF OTHERS

DAY 10

When unbelievers encourage us to "move on" and take care of ourselves or suggest that we deserve better, it is often easy to see the enemy's lies, motivations, and manipulations through their words. We stand firm; crisis averted.

Then along comes a believer appearing to walk steadfast in the ways. Maybe this believer is someone older and more seasoned in scripture, or maybe it's someone who calls themselves a "mature Christian". They don't use the same "moving on" words, but their opinion still causes you to question your stand. Perhaps they may even say words like what is found in 1 Kings 13:18, *"An angel spoke to me ..."* You thought you heard God clearly, but maybe this person knows more? Or maybe God has given this person a message for you? After all, it looks like they've been doing this Jesus-walk much longer than you.

This exact scenario played out in 1 Kings 13. I urge you to read it and see how seriously God takes His call to stand firm on His directive and on His promises. Read how important it is to remain unwavering. In 1 Kings 13:7-9, the man of God passed the first test and remained committed to God's direction because the invitation to do otherwise clearly came by way of a person not walking in the ways of the Lord. Crisis averted.

When the old prophet entered the story, the man of God abandoned his allegiance to God's direction and believed in the deceit of the old prophet. He never sought God's discernment of the information set before him. The man let his own obedience and alignment under God's authority to be influenced by the perceived wisdom or authority of another.

Then God used this same old prophet, who deceived the man, as the one to cast the judgement in the story,

> *You rebelled against the Lord's command and did*
> *not keep the command that Lord God*
> *commanded you–your corpse will never reach the*
> *grave of your fathers.*

— 1 KINGS 13:22

That's a significant punishment, for sure. The Bible never blatantly says why the old prophet deceived the man of God. I think the Lord placed a test in front of the man of God. Just like God does with us when we have people and circumstances arrive in our lives that cause us to question our faith, trust, perseverance, endurance, reliance upon God and, above all, our commitment to follow Him and His directions above all else. That old prophet could be a Christian friend, family member, co-worker, member of a private social media group, or even an inanimate object you perceive as a sign. It also could be that pastor or ministry leader with thousands of likes and followers.

Take your situation to God before you assign any significance to another person's influence into your life, especially if you allow it to move you from the point God has ordained you to be in this season. The "stand" we take to pray, fast and wait upon the Lord for a particular promise has very little to do with the other people in our lives. It has EVERYTHING to do with obedience to what God has directed us to do. When you're at risk of being deceived into abandoning your position, it is critical that you seek God's discernment above all else, and above everyone else. The Holy Spirit will most assuredly orchestrate people and circumstances in our paths to help us, but we will not know the true intent of that message until we obtain confirmation from the Lord.

REFLECTION QUESTIONS:

1. Is there someone in your life you would listen to and follow, even if that advice ran counter to what you've heard from the Lord?
2. How can you move closer to the Lord in this season of waiting to ensure the voice you hear is the Holy Spirit?
3. Write out these scripture verses and place them on your bathroom mirror, on the dashboard of your car, taped to the back of the tv remote: *"Call to me and I will answer you, and will tell you great and hidden things that you have not known."* (Jeremiah 33:3)

PRAYER PAUSE:

Lord Jesus, I seek your wisdom and discernment above all human voices. Help me to walk in your guidance, understand your ways, even when that means stepping out of my comfort zone. Give me the ability to discern your truths within the words spoken to me by others. Convict me to cast off what is not of you, while embracing what is. Convict me of those people I have elevated above your place in my heart, trusting in their opinions and guidance before confirming all with you. Convict me of seeking out that which I desire above that which is best for me, according to your will for my life. Holy Spirit, help me to repent of all these convictions shown to me. Jesus, I seek you above all others. Amen.

ASK...SEEK...KNOCK...BUT DON'T GET YOUR HOPES UP

DAY 11

Did you know there are no "false starts" in God's ministry of reconciliation? God does nothing falsely or without purpose. This journey we are on is much like an earthquake, which never just happens, but is forewarned by little tremors leading up to the big shake.

Breakthrough into marital restoration, a prodigal returning, or any other promise we stand upon comes in little repeated tremors, which are orchestrated by God to chisel our characters, break down our preconceived beliefs and realign our postures under His authority. When we choose to focus on the result, we miss out on the moments God will partner with us along the way. Actually, let me rephrase that: when we choose to focus on the result, God will purposely delay the big restoration until it becomes less important than the relationship He is seeking to build with us.

The Bible never says, "Ask, Seek, Knock ... but don't get your hopes up too high." Don't get your hopes up for them to change. Don't get your hopes up for the marriage to be restored, for that new job, for that new home. Don't get your hopes up for God to work a miracle. How many times have we brought our requests to God, and yet later, we utter phrases like, "I guess it was a false start" or "if I don't hope, then I won't be disappointed". The enemy wins when we perpetuate those words of hidden doubt and discouragement.

We need to silence the enemy's covert call to doubt and question and instead rise to God's calling of HOPE in our lives and pray that for others, even when it defies our limited view and understanding. Hope, even when it counters what you see in front of you. Hope, even when those around you say it's impossible. Our hope should never be placed in sinful, jacked up humans. Our hope rests upon and resides in the almighty, ever-present, all-knowing, resurrecting, miracle-producing power of Jesus.

Now, Lord, what do I wait for? My HOPE is in you.

— PSALMS 39:7

Now may the God of HOPE fill you with all joy and peace as you believe so that you may overflow with HOPE by the power of the Holy Spirit.

— ROMANS 15:13

Now faith is the reality of what is HOPED for, the proof of what is not seen.

— HEBREWS 11:1

This HOPE will not disappoint us, because God's love has been poured out in our hearts through the Holy Spirit who was given to us.

— ROMANS 5:5

We have this HOPE as an anchor for the soul, firm and secure. It enters the inner sanctuary behind the curtain.

— HEBREWS 6:19

I know the plans I have for you–this is the Lord's declaration–plans for your well-being, not for disaster to give you a future and a HOPE.

— JEREMIAH 29:11

REFLECTION QUESTIONS:

1. When was the last time you remember saying, "don't get your hopes up"? What were the circumstances that triggered that response? Did not getting your hopes up actually help you?
2. When you read the scripture verses about hope, which one speaks to your situation today?
3. Did you know the Bible includes 365 verses specifically addressing hope? Make it a goal to memorize one verse of hope each week of the year, starting today.

PRAYER PAUSE:

Jesus, I know this journey is a work in progress, but I often feel so lacking in hope. I am afraid to get my hopes up because in my mind, the disappointment won't hurt as much. But that itself is a lie of the enemy meant to keep me in bondage, to keep me from praising and experiencing your joy, even as I learn to wait patiently for you to move. My hope resides in you, not in another person's decisions or actions. My hope anchored in you will not disappoint me, because your love has been poured out to help me through the Holy Spirit. You know the plans you have for me–plans for my well-being, not for my disaster, to give me a future and a hope. Lord Jesus, I will hold on to this hope as an anchor for my soul. It is in your name; I pray. Amen.

WAITING WELL CHANGES EVERYTHING

IS THIS YOUR RED SEA MOMENT? ARE YOU FEELING LIKE THE ISRAELITES?

DAY 12

Even though the Israelites were guided by God's pillar of cloud by day and a pillar of fire by night, they didn't walk up to the Red Sea overflowing with faith, singing and praising the wonder of their God. They were angry, complaining to Moses, and scared for their lives.

> *What have you done to us by bringing us out of Egypt?... It would have been better for us to serve the Egyptians than to die in the wilderness.*
>
> — EXODUS 14:11-12

They couldn't see that the dead end in front of them was actually about to become their launching point into freedom, all perfectly orchestrated by God.

> *Then the Lord spoke to Moses, 'Tell the Israelites to turn back and camp in front of Pi-hahiroth, between Migdol and the sea, you must camp in front of Baal-zephon, facing it by the sea.*
>
> — EXODUS 14:1-2

Wouldn't you think if God was giving them the exact physical markers of where to set up camp, it would be in a secret, secluded hiding place not to be found by Pharaoh? It's like being given a street address or GPS coordinates from God as He says, "Recalculate ... I want you to stay the night HERE" and then you learn He's given the same address to thieves.

Pi-hahiroth was a range of mountains with caves. Migdol means a fortress or tower, while some scholars believe Migdol was referring to another mountain range. Either way, to their right and to their left were large barriers and to their backs was the Red Sea. God directed Moses to lead them into a literal dead end. They were trapped in a valley with no way to retreat, as the Egyptian army closed in, eager to re-capture and enslave them. But why?

God guided them into a physical dead end and God planned the hardening of Pharaoh's heart to chase after them because it was His plan to deliver them! The miracle of the Red Sea parting had purpose!!

God used those circumstances to show the Israelites that He was to be trusted, He would provide, and that there was no physical barrier they saw as impossible, which God could not overcome. He literally parted the Red Sea, not to save them from death, but to provide an opportunity for them to see His power and glory manifested in a way they could never have predicted, nor accomplished, on their own.

God orchestrated ALL of it so that the Israelites had an opportunity to stand on the other side of the trial with the assurance that God was to be trusted. He would provide. NOTHING was beyond his capacity. Today, God uses your situation to remind you of the same. Generations later, HE IS STILL THE ONE orchestrating it all. He is still to be trusted. He will provide. And NOTHING is beyond his capacity to heal, manifest, or move.

> *But now, thus says the Lord, your Creator, "Do not fear, for I have redeemed you; I have called you by name; you are Mine! When you pass through the waters, I will be with you; and through the rivers, they will not overwhelm you when you walk through the fire, you will not be scorched, nor will the flame burn you. Do not fear, for I am with you; I will bring your offspring from the east and gather you from the west.*
>
> — ISAIAH 43:1-2, 5

REFLECTION QUESTIONS:

1. Do you have a Red Sea moment? If you look back on it with discerning eyes and Holy Spirit guidance, how can you see God's orchestration and divine set up, reminding you He is to be trusted and He will provide?

2. When is the last time you've said, "wow, that's a coincidence"? Did you know that coincidence is a worldly term for the unexplainable movements of God? Coincidence doesn't exist in the Bible. How were God's hands moving in your life and through those circumstances?

PRAYER PAUSE:

God, I now understand that you're using these difficult circumstances to show me that you are to be trusted, you will provide, and that there is no barrier impossible for you to overcome. It doesn't matter whether the trials are triggered by the enemy because you reign above it all. You've allowed these moments to transform me. Amid all this pain, you are seeking to move me from the place I've settled into. I can trust you to work out all the details that are beyond my own direct control. As for me, I will refocus my eyes to change that which is in my control–the words I choose, the actions I take, the choices I make. Holy Spirit, convict me of the need for repentance in all areas where I have fallen short. It's in Jesus' name, I pray.

_____

_____

_____

_____

_____

_____

SO MUCH SAID AND DONE...

DAY 13

I just don't think God can fix all that, or maybe He can but just doesn't want to.

I just don't think ...

Did you know what you think is a subtle, but clear, window into the condition of your heart? Under a shroud of reasons why someone doubts is the very real struggle to believe God IS who He says He is. We don't like to call it what it actually is but unbelief is at the core. If I am a lukewarm fence sitter in God's Kingdom, and I doubt God's ability or His willingness to move, heal, and provide, then I inevitably create a gap of space between me and Him. Ohhh, how the enemy loves even a hairline gap to slither within.

When the Israelites were following Moses to the Promised Land, they doubted God many times, and it never ended well for them. They doubted God's ability to provide food; they doubted His ability to protect them from enemies; they even doubted the blessings awaiting them in the Promised Land. All those doubts cost them massively, and not just 39 additional years of camping. It also canceled the opportunity for their own generation to experience the blessings of that new land, which God promised to Abraham long before. Their children would step into and receive the blessing, but not the parents. There are serious consequences to doubting God ... time delayed, blessings denied, even plans changed.

Doubt even appeared within the Disciples of the New Testament, and Jesus didn't mince words when addressing it.

> *Later, Jesus appeared to the Eleven themselves as they were reclining at the table. He rebuked their unbelief and hardness of heart, because they did not believe those who saw Him after he had risen.*
>
> — MARK 16:14 CSB

Jesus didn't just chastise His own Disciples because they doubted whether others had seen Him after rising from the dead; He called out and rebuked their unbelief. How many times have you voiced, "This isn't going to happen" or "It can't change" or "It can't be fixed"? What if your own words, judgements, and unbelief are the very barriers to your prayers being answered?

Read Mark 6:4-5. Jesus was back in His hometown, surrounded by everything and everyone that was familiar to Him. The one place where everyone knew Him was the one place Jesus was NOT able to do a miracle, except heal a few sick people. Scripture says, HE WAS AMAZED AT THEIR UNBELIEF. What if the degree of their unbelief is equal to what is hidden in the deep recesses of your heart?

Personally, I had to sit on this for a while. I never thought anything could hinder Jesus from breaking through with a miracle, least of all anything I placed as a barrier. How powerful are my words? What blockages are my judgements of situations and people, saying they can't change? Scripture warns us that there is enough power in that unbelief to actually hinder the healing efforts of the ONLY one who can make that miracle happen.

We need to be very clear here ... this is not some kind of spiritual, positive affirmation on your part ... putting "positive vibes into the universe" hoping for random positive returns. This is pure, untainted, unwavering belief in Jesus, who moves mountains, heals the sick, restores relationships, and defies the impossible. It's not a difficult process, but it is a heart process.

I had to surrender my continual obsession with control, needing to analyze and come to conclusions on every detail of what is said and done in my life. I had to release that I didn't actually know what was going on, even though my mind and pride liked to tell me that I did. I had to seek forgiveness each and every time doubt ... no, let's call it what it is ... unbelief came into my mind. And, I had to take a deep dive into reading God's Word because the only thing that erases unbelief is Truth found in His Word. Truth like this:

> *But let him ask in faith without doubting. For the doubter is like the surging sea, driven and tossed by the wind.*
>
> — JAMES 1:6

> *Truly I tell you, if anyone says to this mountain, 'Be lifted up and thrown into the sea' and does not doubt in his heart, but believes that what he says will happen, it will be done for him.*
>
> — MARK 11:23

> *He (Abraham) did not waver in unbelief at God's promise but was strengthened in his faith and gave glory to God.*
>
> — ROMANS 4:20

> *With God, ALL things are possible.*
>
> — MATTHEW 19:26

REFLECTION QUESTIONS:

1. Is there a situation in your life right now that you may have spoken doubt over? One of the strongest ways to combat doubt is to pray as the situation should be, not as you see it today. What would your prayer sound like if you began praying for how that situation will be in the future, after God has moved?
2. Have you often felt like you're floating in the surging sea of a situation, driven and tossed by the wind? Is there doubt and unbelief hidden in the recess of your heart or are you anchored on the rock of His Word?

3. Nothing is impossible with God. All things are possible with God. While the Gospels declare this truth, do you feel a twinge of doubt when reading those words? Does your mind quickly flash to a person or situation that smacks of this truth? Those quick glimpses into your heart are the very places to focus your prayers, seeking healing, clarity and surrender of your own judgements.

PRAYER PAUSE:

It's time to get real and vomit the doubt. Honesty in prayer reaps the greatest benefit. Use your journal to write each doubt that looms in your mind. Need extra space? Grab another piece of paper. The Holy Spirit can only guide you to the extent you're willing to surrender. After writing all the doubts filling your mind, place it inside your Bible. In other words, physically give it to God. When more doubts come to mind, go back and write them down, too. Then begin praying with your now emptied spirit of all that doubt. Surrender your need for control, the need to analyze and draw conclusions on every detail of what is said and done in your life. Release the need to know what is going on, what that other person is doing, even though your mind and pride tell you otherwise. And seek forgiveness for the ways of the past, seek strength to walk in this new way, and seek wisdom to see when old habits are looming. Pray all of this in Jesus' name.

_____

_____

_____

_____

WHY? WHY? WHY?!

DAY 14

How would you like to set out on a trip to receive something God has promised you and know it's going to take 11 days to get there, but 40 years later, you're still walking it out, wandering and wondering when you'll see this promise to fruition?

Such was the case with Moses and God's people, grumbling, questioning and wandering in the wilderness, seeking to settle on the piece of real estate that God said was theirs to claim. Yet, their attitudes and behaviors required constant recalculating, traveling 40 years to a destination that could have been reached in less than two weeks.

Don't miss the point here. Attitudes matter. Their impatience led to creating and worshiping false gods, taking their eyes off the one true God, doubting the voice of God, even grumbling about the manna they were provided by God every morning! Their list of grievances against Him for everything not right in their lives was long. Their attitudes were clear, as they often voiced, "We were better off in our old life."

I wonder if they asked as many times as I have asked, "Why?!?" One little question with such big implications. Why is it happening this way? Why the pain? Why the wait? Why, Why, WHY?! I fell asleep contemplating this question.

In the middle of the night, I tossed and turned in the darkness sensing the word Deuteronomy hanging heavy in the air above me. I'd love to say I knew immediately of the significance, but honestly, it's not a book of the Bible I knew well. Sleep obviously wasn't coming until I got up and started reading, so I randomly opened to the book, confident the Holy Spirit would meet me wherever I landed.

In Deuteronomy 8, Moses was speaking words of warning, guidance and authority over Israel's young adults, as they stood at the literal edge of their parent's promised land. The generation that witnessed the Red Sea parting would not be the ones placing their feet onto the new Promised Land. Their disbelief and disobedient behaviors denied the parents of the blessing that would now come only to their children. It was here that I unpacked the answer to my question of "why".

> *... Remember that God led you on the entire journey these 40 years in the wilderness so that he might humble you and test you to know what was in your heart, whether or not you would keep his commands.*
>
> — DEUTERONOMY 8:2

Just like the Israelites, God is leading me. He goes before me on this journey. I am not alone. He humbles me and knows what is in my heart. It's been a long season already; God, please don't make it forty years. You want to know if I'm going to obey your directives and commands? While I know I've certainly done a stellar job at failing to obey in the past, this time will be different.

> *...He humbled you by letting you go hungry; then he gave you manna to eat, so that you might learn that man does not live on bread alone but on every word that comes from God.*
>
> — DEUTERONOMY 8:3

He is humbling me by letting me go a season of time without that which I desire, so that I learn to lean upon His Word for my nourishment. He will provide what my body needs but not at the expense of what my soul needs. I've been trying to fill a hunger that God wants to soul satisfy with Himself. Are there things I have desired more than Him?

> *...So keep the commands of the Lord your God by walking in his ways and fearing Him. For God is bringing you into a good land. A land where you will eat food without shortage, where you will lack nothing.*
>
> — DEUTERONOMY 8:6-7, 9

Right now, it's hard to imagine a time when I'll be standing within a promise fulfilled rather than looking with anticipation from afar. I start by moving my eyes off the circumstances, off the dysfunction, to focus squarely on God. Repenting daily. Forgiving hourly. Loving despite the circumstances. I know fulfillment of a promise sought through prayer is not contingent upon my "works" but the alignment of my heart with God. This promise requires a transformation of my heart, not a to-do list of my actions, and by faithfully abiding, I will obtain the promise and lack nothing.

> *...You may say to yourself, "My power and my own ability have gained this wealth for me," but remember that the Lord your God gives you the power to gain wealth, in order to confirm his covenant he swore to your fathers, as it is today.*
>
> — DEUTERONOMY 8:17

Uggghhhh, God ... now we're digging deep and exposing my greatest prideful weaknesses, taking credit where it is only yours to own. How many times have I assumed responsibility for the blessings you've provided? How many times have I seen a movement toward that promise fulfilled and pridefully assumed it was all me? God forgive my prideful arrogance and remind me daily that you, who giveth, also takes away when not used as you intend.

> *...Understand that God is not giving this good land (the thing you prayed for) to possess because of your righteousness.*

— DEUTERONOMY 9:6

...Keep every command I am giving you today, so that you may have the strength to cross into and possess the land you are to inherit. And do that so you may live long in the land the Lord promised.

— DEUTERONOMY 11:8

...it is a land the Lord cares for. He is always watching over it from the beginning to the end of the year.

— DEUTERONOMY 11:12

From beginning to end ... from before the implosion or the dysfunction to after His transformation ... He is always watching over and caring. These words are like Neosporin to my wounded soul.

My middle of the night, God-inspired, answers to "why" have me hungry for more of Him and humbled by His sovereignty. I am acutely aware and appreciative of all He has walked me through, and I stand confidently in this season of waiting upon Him. I love that His answers to our questions are not stoic "Because I said so." Rather, through His Word, I am deeply saturated in nourishment that truly makes waiting well change everything.

REFLECTION QUESTIONS:

1. How long has your journey been? Have you really let it resonate in your soul that God is the one leading you through this difficult time? Do you think your attitude has lengthened or shortened the journey?
2. What are your questions of why? Lay them before God in prayer and allow His responses to fill your soul.

WAITING WELL CHANGES EVERYTHING

NAVIGATING THE EXILE

DAY 15

There are moments in life when we feel like we're in an "exile," not separated from God, but certainly waiting on God. The promises He's tucked in our hearts seem on hold, and we're playing a waiting game while He works out the details. So what do we do in an exile? Our tendency is to retreat from life. We grab some comfort food, binge watch and probably do lots of crying.

In those times of walking within the wilderness, when we need something to grasp onto, Jeremiah 29:11 anchors and assures us that God indeed has *"plans for us, plans for our well-being, not for disaster, to give us a future and a hope."* But let's take a few steps back and look at the context and some truths about this season of exile and wilderness found in the scriptures written before verse 11.

Jeremiah 29:1, 4 & 7 ... While King Nebuchadnezzar had deported God's chosen people from Jerusalem to Babylon in exile, the Lord made it clear through Jeremiah's prophetic letter to the Israelites, that God alone, arranged the deportation of His people. I always skipped that inconspicuous little detail, focusing more on the exile itself. There are two huge gems worthy of excavation,

1. it's critical to not just understand, but ACCEPT, that our loving Heavenly Father will sometimes bring us to uncomfortable places for our own good, although, there's nothing that feels good at the time, and
2. we often cast blame at the person or the situation causing our pain instead of considering there is a spiritual aspect that we can't visibly see.

The Israelites, no doubt, looked at King Nebuchadnezzar as the source of their pain and suffering. He received their wrath because he was the one they could visibly see. He was the one who uprooted them, who forced them from their homes, and radically altered their lifestyles. He was the issue. But God told the Israelites twice that HE deported them. The God they worshipped. The God they couldn't see. Their loving God orchestrated in the spiritual realm an exile in the physical realm. Please don't miss this ... what we see in a situation is never the clear reflection of what is truly going on.

Jeremiah 29:5 & 6 ... Accept the fact that you're going to be in this season for a while. Before God told the Israelites how long they'd be in exile, He gave them His expectations:

> *Build houses and live in them. Plant gardens and eat their produce. Find wives for yourselves, and have sons and daughters. Multiply there; do not decrease.*
>
> — JEREMIAH 29:5-6

Build a house? Plant a garden? Have kids? These were all long-term directives for a place the Israelites didn't want to be in. Our seasons of exile or wilderness will all look different, and I'm praying that they won't last the 70 years of the Israelites, but what I can tell you is the longer you fight it, the longer you will be planted there. Leaning into all that God has to show you and surrendering to His transformative ways will insure the greatest breakthrough in the least amount of time.

Jeremiah 29:7 ... Inhale, exhale and accept it.

> *"Pursue the well being of the city I have deported you to. Pray to the Lord on its behalf, for when it thrives, you thrive."*
>
> — JEREMIAH 29:7

I can imagine how hard it was for the Israelites to pray for the king and all those who persecuted them hourly. But God was calling them to bless their captors, and so are we called to bless those who have blocked, persecuted, and hurt us. God says, when we pray for them and they thrive, then we thrive. How counter intuitive is that?! Only you and God know who should be the focus of your prayers in the exile. It's hard to swallow at first, but God massively blesses and extends peace upon those who can rise up and pray for the souls of those doing the persecuting.

Jeremiah 29:8 & 9 ... You're searching YouTube and Facebook for prophetic words from ANYONE. You're seeking advice from friends and family. You're desperate for a sign, a dream, anything to give you direction. Warning! When we are desperate for a word,

ANY word will often suffice. And the world is all too willing to supply those words:

> "You need to move on."
> "God wouldn't want you suffering like this."
> "Are you sure you heard God right?"

God knew we would go seeking, that's why He gave his declaration in verses 8 and 9.

> *Don't be deceived; don't go seeking dream interpretations; don't go seeking advice, for they are prophesying FALSELY to you in my name. I HAVE NOT SENT THEM.*
>
> — JEREMIAH 29:8-9 *(EMPHASIS ADDED)*

Jeremiah 29:10 & 11 ... So often we glorify verse 11 but we miss the fact that God, in verse 10, had just announced that the Israelites were to be in exile for almost a lifetime–70 years to be exact. When God spoke of knowing the plans in verse 11, He was reassuring His people that despite the length of the exile, and the pain and suffering of the exile, He had a plan. A plan for their well-being, not for disaster, to give them a future and a hope beyond the exile. He was reassuring them that, in this exile, they can call out to Him, pray and seek Him, and that they will be heard by and find Him. And that God planned to restore their fortunes and their relationships from the place HE banished them to.

In the midst of what feels like an exile or wilderness season, there is no greater or sweeter words than God saying,

> *I will restore you to the place from which I deported you.*
>
> —JEREMIAH 29:14B

We are encouraged to anchor ourselves on faith in an exile and know that faith always proceeds the evidence of God's plan, which is most assuredly on the way.

REFLECTION QUESTIONS:

1. Do you feel trapped in an exile season? Are there people or circumstances you would point to as the "cause" of your exile? Begin praying for the Holy Spirit to show you what you are to learn and how you can transform in this period.
2. In what ways may God want you to bless those people you see as the cause of your situation?
3. Are there people in your life whom you may have allowed greater influence to speak into your circumstances than what God would want?

PRAYER PAUSE:

Remember that God will not transform you into the person He designed you to be, only to return you to the original dysfunctional circumstances. God was seeking to transform the Israelites' faith before He returned them to their homeland. And He will do the same for you through a surrendered heart. Begin praying BOLDLY for God's Will to manifest in your life and the lives of those around you. Move beyond focusing your prayers on the circumstances you see now, but rather pray on the details after the restoration occurs. What will it be like? How will things be different? What will YOU do differently in the new season of restoration? Pray for that! Thank God and give glory and praise to Him before it all happens!

I WAS A WATER BUG, SKIMMING ALONG THE SURFACE OF LIFE'S POND

DAY 16

Why and how did I become so manipulated into thinking "moving on" would provide me with joy, contentment, and peace rather than trusting in God's sovereignty over the situation? My faith resembled a water bug, skimming along the surface of the pond on a hot, muggy day. Every so often, I'd dip under the surface to grab a bite of nourishment to sustain me. There was no real commitment to the relationship that God sought with and for me, which was only to be found by diving deep within the waters. The Bible was a book I rarely opened and definitely struggled to understand. Tithing was a $20 put into a basket, motivated more by my guilt than obedience. And praying? Well, that was more of a check-in to make sure God aligned Himself with the plans I had made for myself.

So, when the enemy came to steal marital territory, I was far from battle ready. My choices to elevate my kids, my career, my marriage, and my prideful independence above my relationship with God played a direct and life altering cause and effect for the future. Now I can see the enemy does a stellar job at creating a false appearance that there is peace, joy, contentment, and new beginnings on the other side of "moving on".

We look to the future and project our hopes upon the closure of a heart-wrenching situation, but in reality, all we do is surrender more territory to the enemy. He doesn't want us to see that peace, joy, and contentment result when we surrender and become obedient to God, when we surrender our will and pick up the commitment to follow God's will (no matter how hard it is). Through Jesus' sacrifice on the cross, we break the enemy's chains. We bust open the prison doors and walk out into this incredible relationship, even during uncertainty, instability, and the unknown. It all is possible by first getting our own priorities, relationships, and heart aligned properly with God.

After our divorce, when I thought I was "moving on", God had other plans for me. The moving on I've done is actually moving into a deep, eternity-cemented relationship with God, and not at all about "moving on" from my husband or my marriage.

Over these last seven years, the Holy Spirit has spoken directly to me, and through other people, and within dreams to relay six significant messages:

Let's put us back together, spoken by my husband during one of several tremors to restoration.

I've given you the end of the story; are you going to trust me in how you get there? Spoken by a Christian mentor, minutes after silently praying for God to speak through her to me.

Time will be stolen, but I am protecting your relationship, spoken by the Holy Spirit when asking for wisdom and discernment about a dream of being in an antique store where a pocket watch was missing, but gold wedding bands were sitting out in public sight.

For your children's children, spoken by the Holy Spirit while stirring spaghetti at the stove one night, with the explanation that the years of standing had far more impact than simply a marriage restoration. Generations would benefit.

See? See? If I had given you what you wanted, this journey would not have happened, spoken by the Holy Spirit while washing dishes one night.

You are birthing something new, provided as an explanation by the Holy Spirit, after a dream in which my husband announced I was pregnant (I'm loooong past that phase of life!).

Before you read this and think, Wow, I wish I heard from God that much! Consider that six messages were received over seven years. That's a great deal of quiet in between significant holy interactions. How did I survive the long periods of quiet? Those encounters with God became my signposts, the indicators of God's presence, as spoken in Jeremiah ...

> *Set up road markers for yourself; establish signposts!*
> *Keep the highway in mind, the way you have traveled.*
>
> — JEREMIAH 31:21

When the enemy says life around me is as uncertain as quicksand, each one of these Holy Spirit moments ground me in truth.

When reflecting on my past choices and perspectives, I can now see I missed the mark on everything. Seriously, I was so far off base, yet I was so confident that I had it all figured out. When you're acting like a water bug in constant motion across the pond of life, how can God ever meet you, use you, and minister to you if you don't slow down and deliberately go deep for nourishment?

> *Call to me, and I will answer you, and show you great and mighty things, which you do not know.*
>
> — JEREMIAH 33:3

When you self-determine and think you know what's best for you, confident that "moving on" in your strength and determination means freedom from today's pain, it gives no margin in your life for God to show you otherwise. God has your very own personalized messages, signposts, and indicators waiting; He has "great and mighty" things to show you. They arrive after you take a big breath and do a deeper dive into a relationship with Him. Cease the desire to "move on". Instead, choose to move INTO a life-altering, game changing relationship with God and watch it transform everything around you and within you.

REFLECTION QUESTIONS:

1. Can you identify ways that you may have been that water bug skimming on the pond of life?

2. Can you remember a time when you thought you had it all figured out? You knew the precise reason behind someone or something's occurrence only to realize later that you completely missed the mark? Did you welcome God into that discernment to show you "great and mighty things"? Or was it by your own understanding?
3. What are the signposts, markers, or messages you've received during your journey to show God is within this difficult season? Do you reflect upon those when waves of frustration and impatience arrive?

_____

_____

_____

_____

_____

_____

_____

_____

_____

_____

_____

_____

_____

_____

IGNORING THE RED FLAGS

DAY 17

According to Investopedia, the definition of a red flag is a warning signal pointing to a potential problem or threat that warrants further investigation.

My past is littered with the tattered red flags of warnings I chose to ignore. Times when I blatantly passed over God's voice alerting me to interactions with people or circumstances that were not His best for me. Ignoring red flags is really easy to do when your heart is not aligned under God's authority, when you are not obedient and surrendered to Him, and when you're skimming the surface of faith.

In past relationships, I ignored red flags which appeared through sudden angry explosions and hurtful words spoken to me. I looked beyond the presence of pornography. I disregarded clear evidence of competing "attractions". With self-confidence that I could change any situation, I waged a determined effort to climb over or break down other people's emotional walls and reduce emotional distancing. Hindsight is such a powerful teacher.

Today, I can see those red flags flapping in the winds of my past. I now recognize, through the guidance of the Holy Spirit, when those moments of warning and caution were clearly disregarded and totally discarded. I was prideful and independently confident that I could make it all work.

The world would sympathize by saying I did the best that I could do with the information I had in front of me. I say, Baloney! I maintained a surface level relationship with God and all my decisions flowed through that choice. Encountering red flags without a relationship with Jesus means you're the one defining the significance of a potential threat. You're the one trying to decipher if the moment of alarm is worthy of your attention or if you should just ignore it. Blaring sirens may go off, but yet, they can also be silenced by our own desires to "keep the peace," not "making a mountain out of a molehill," or the one on repeat in my head ... "you made your bed, now quietly lay in it."

When you have an obedient, right-standing relationship under God's authority, red flags become times for pause and prayer. There's a peaceful realization that God has it all worked out, so you don't need to push or manipulate the circumstances in your own strength.

This is a good place to stop and clarify the difference between influences from the enemy and God. Under the enemy's influence, I should feel guilt and shame for missing the red flags, and even go so far as to condemn myself for sucking at decision-making in general. I should carry that luggage of regret for a lifetime, reminding me of the weight and consequences of my choices. But, with Jesus as my Savior, the Holy Spirit convicts and extends mercy and grace as I step into a deeper level of freedom through repentance. I can trust God's guidance when red flags happen in the future and seek His wisdom and discernment for how to proceed. I can wait well because I have the confidence, faith, and trust that God is in the details. He already knows what red flags are coming before I do.

REFLECTION QUESTIONS:

1. Ask the Holy Spirit to show you times and areas of your life when red flags were present, but you purposefully overlooked and ignored them.
2. What was the condition of your heart and connection to God in those times? Seek forgiveness from God for each time that you ignored the red flags placed in front of you.
3. In the future, what will you do differently when encountering red flags?

PRAYER PAUSE:

Lord, thank You for the gift of hindsight and for how you use it to remind me of your faithfulness. Every red flag I breezed right by was a moment in which I unknowingly was met by your mercy and grace. Help me now to be so deeply in love with you that future red flags are not even a debate. Give me wisdom and discernment and enable me to unwaveringly trust your guidance. It is in your name, Jesus, that I pray. Amen.

THE ONE WITHOUT SIN CASTS THE FIRST STONE...

DAY 18

The Pharisees (the religious authorities in Jesus' day) had brought attention to a woman caught in the act of adultery. They devised a theological trap. If Jesus denied this woman's sin and public death penalty by stoning, it would also mean He denied the religious law established by God through Moses. They waited with great anticipation, convinced they had Him cornered, sure that this would be the successful set-up to bring an end to His growing influence.

He, who has no sin, Jesus said, let them be the first to throw the rock, cast the judgment, and condemn this woman. Whoa! I can sense their complete disappointment when Jesus balanced the scales of judgement by introducing grace and mercy. As I read this account in John 8, it was easy for me to criticize the Pharisees for their self-righteous religiosity and cheer at Jesus' brilliant response. But then I wondered if among the crowd of Pharisees were also the married partners wronged in this adulterous act. The Bible didn't say if there was a husband of the adulterous woman or a wife of the adulterous man present. If there was, did THEY get to cast stones? Didn't they have a greater stake in this punishment than the Pharisees? Weren't they collateral damage in this marital meltdown and deserving of retribution?

The desire to pick up a "stone" and lodge harsh words or physical actions towards someone who was or is contributing to your marital dysfunction is normal. But what we do with that desire is critical, as it often leads to the hardening of our hearts from accumulated bitterness, anger, and resentment.

Empathy is often hard to muster on our own until Jesus enters the equation. While you may struggle with a spouse navigating a foot in each family unit (double minded in all their ways, as written in James 1), the "other" person may see you as a barrier to the happiness they seek. While you stand for eventual restoration and reconciliation, this "other" person may come to terms with months or even years spent in a relationship that will not play out as they hoped and dreamed. No matter how many posts on social media manufacture an appearance of happiness, it's a safe bet that life as the "other" has not been what they had hoped when becoming involved with your spouse. This is a good place to stop and avoid an embittered, "Good!" The enemy is in overdrive, creating chaos, pain, and suffering on all fronts. Your enemy is NOT your spouse or the "other" person. It's not flesh and bone (Ephesians 6:12) but there is a spiritual battle underway, a battle in which you only see the surface level dysfunctions rather than the underlying tactics and strategies.

When we allow God to transform our lives, we surrender to a deep and all-encompassing relationship with the Lord. We have a heavenly Father who draws us under His wing, who bandages our wounds, who provides everything we and our children need. Empathy, grace, and mercy are reflected in us because of our walk with Jesus. This other person may have never known the unconditional love of God. They may have never opened a Bible and read the truth. Or maybe they go to church; maybe they claim they're a follower of Jesus, even though all actions indicate otherwise. Remember, in all these scenarios, they are separated from God and are an unsuspecting pawn in the hands of the enemy.

In this battle, grace and mercy are powerful defenders of hearts, and prayer is the weapon of choice:

Jesus Christ of Nazareth, who came in the flesh, I thank you so very much for opening my eyes to what really matters to you. My heart aligned with you is far more valuable in eternity than what I temporarily seek on earth. Thank you for never turning your back on me in my own disobedience. Thank you for that unconditional love of your Father. We are all prodigals at one point or another, and so I pray for this "other" person right now. Lord, I ask you to bind up every evil influence present in this situation, and in the lives of my spouse and this person and cast them where you so choose. In the void of those evil influences, overwhelm the situation and every cell of their bodies with the Holy Spirit. Allow your light and truth to reach every dark corner. Cancel every scheme and lie meant to distract each of them from your truth. Remove the scales and open their eyes to your loving grace and mercy. Heal those deep soul wounds within each of them that only you are aware of. God, if that other person has a spouse of their own, divorced or not, I ask you to stir an undeniable calling to you, begin a restoration process in their original family unit. Place Godly men and women in each of their paths to speak truth into their life and their own spouses. Restore their marriage and family in your glory. Bring blessing and testimony upon their restored family unit.

Lord, I do not know all the ways to pray for this person, but your Holy Spirit hears my groanings and intercedes on my behalf. Take the intentions of my heart and cover this other person with needed prayers. Stir a longing within them for a deep relationship with you. Call them to repentance. Call them to you. And lastly, Lord, I know that you usually do not override a person's free will. You want that return to be of their own decision. When Jonah sought to flee in the opposite directions of your call on his life, you did not interfere in his free will to choose. But you altered the surrounding circumstances to apply pressure on his life because of his choice to be disobedient. I thank you for that pressure in my own life, which always draws me back to you. I pray for a mighty discontent, distaste, and dissatisfaction in my spouse's life for anything that is not of you, and not your best in their life, and I pray this for myself. Alter the circumstances to apply just the amount of pressure for each of us to turn our heads upwards to you, to change our postures to one of surrender and obedience. Your Will be done. We are not worthy of you, but you call us worthy. I cannot seek your forgiveness and expect the freedom of chains to break if I am not willing to forgive others. Convict me of any roots of anger and bitterness that have taken hold within my heart. Through repentance, help me stay clean of all negative emotions so that I may be a clear window through which others can see you. It's in Jesus' name and the power of His crucified and resurrected body that I pray. Amen.

It's so important to remember that God's directive to love, even those who have hurt us, is about the condition of our own heart and alignment under God's authority. Praying for those who have hurt us is actually an act of our own surrender that breaks chains of bondage and opens the door to our own freedom. It pushes back darkness and allows the light of Jesus to move over and through the circumstances. We pray in obedience, not motivated to receive blessings, but oh, how our loving Heavenly Father blesses our obedience to care for others, even those who appear to be against us.

> *When they (the Pharisees) heard this, they left one by one, starting with the older men. Only he was left, with the woman in the center. When Jesus stood up, he said to her, "Woman, where are they? Has no one condemned you?" "No one, Lord," she answered. "Neither do I condemn you," said Jesus. "Go, and from now on do not sin anymore."*
>
> — JOHN 8: 9-11

> *If you do not stand firm in your faith, then you will not stand at all.*
>
> — ISAIAH 7:9

For if you forgive other people for their offenses, your Heavenly Father will also forgive you.

— MATTHEW 6:14

SEE? SEE?! IF I HAD GIVEN YOU WHAT YOU WANTED...

DAY 19

On a random night, a few years into this standing journey, I was at the kitchen sink washing a pot, not really thinking about anything. Suddenly this voice spoke from behind me. "See? See? If I had given you what you wanted when you first prayed for it, this journey would not have happened. All that I've shown you wouldn't have happened. Your endurance and perseverance were refined in this journey."

To say I stood mesmerized by what I had just heard is an understatement. I was overwhelmed by the magnitude of the Spirit washing over me, as I washed that pot.

We get so blinded by everything that is not happening in our timing. We want the end result of prayer. We want out of the unknown, uncomfortable, painful season we're standing in. If we're honest, we want what we want when we want it.

But imagine if God said, "On this particular day, I'm going to do this action because I want you to see how I will provide for you. And during that particular week, you're going to walk through a hard conflict with this certain person because it's going to teach you a lesson you will need for this experience in the future. And beware, that month at the end of the year is really going to test you because I want you to truly feel my protection and my healing. Oh, and during these days, I'm going to orchestrate this person to connect with that person. It won't have anything to do with you directly, but it's necessary for their healing, which will assist with the healing and restoration of that person you have lifted in prayer for a long time."

Are you truly equipped to be in the knowledge of God's plans and purposes for you? To me, it's incredibly exhausting and overwhelming to be told every detail, every reason, every interconnected weaving of God's magnificence. Instead, I now rest peacefully, knowing that He has it all covered, and I don't need the details. That's what anchored faith does for you. Every now and then, God gives me a hint of what He's orchestrating next, all in the beautiful tapestry of His plan and purpose. I don't go seeking to know, but I'm so very grateful that He gifts me with little nuggets of insight along the way. They're like energy drinks in my spirit, boosting and reminding me of His ongoing work on my behalf.

See? See? If God had given you what you wanted, in the timing you wanted, His perfect plan and purpose would not be happening in the way that has been building your faith, building your relationship with Him, and building your testimony for others to see Jesus in you. There's incredible rest, peace, contentment, and joy to be

WAITING WELL CHANGES EVERYTHING

experienced when we wait well knowing that God really has already answered our prayers, even though we can't see all the ways just yet.

> *Blessed is she who believed, for there will be a fulfillment of those things which were told her from the Lord.*
>
> — LUKE 1:45

REFLECTION QUESTIONS:

1. Can you remember a time when the wait for answered prayer illuminated God's hands over the situation? What was your reaction?
2. Have you been overly anxious to know all the details? How can you rest easy within the shelter of God's wing, knowing He has it all figured out?
3. What good advice does Psalms 27:14 give us? Write it on a sticky note and place it on your bathroom mirror or car's dashboard where you can see it often.

_____

_____

_____

_____

_____

THE POWER OF PRAYER AND FASTING, ACCORDING TO JESUS

DAY 20

I never realized the specific instruction for prayer and fasting that Jesus shared with His disciples are not included in some Bible translations. Don't take my word for it. Investigate Mark 9:29 for yourself. The disciples had just asked Jesus why they weren't able to withdraw the evil spirits from the boy. The King James Version states, *"And he said unto them, this kind (of evil spirit) can come forth by nothing, but by prayer and fasting."* The CSB version says, *"And he told them, 'This kind can come out by nothing but prayer.'"* NIV, NLT, ESV, and others state, "Anything but prayer", "only by prayer", and "nothing but prayer". Where's the fasting?

This omission is CRAZY to me! I can attest to the POWER of fasting stated by Jesus. I've completed 10, 12, 21 and 40-day fasts. The clarity, energy, and concentration are incredible! The insights, breakthroughs, and fellowship with God are phenomenal. I used to read of Jesus' 40-day fast in the wilderness and think it was only because of who He was that it could happen. I was so wrong!! It's

God's Living Water and Bread of Life that sustains you. Prayer brings you in close communion with God. Fasting breaks the world's grip on you. The two combined create one of the most AMAZING, POWERFUL experiences you can have in your journey of learning to wait well upon the Lord.

Fasting is also not exclusive to the New Testament. God's people have been fasting as a means of sacrifice, worship, and communication with Him since sin entered the world. God's chosen people fasted before battle, fasted for submission, and fasted to discern His will. Between finding the food, preparing the food and eating the food, meals were an all-encompassing and focused task of life during Biblical times. Fasting meant inactivity for everyone; it meant denying what the flesh craved as a purposed sacrifice to God. Today, it takes five minutes to microwave a full meal, but we'll sit for eight hours and binge a hobby, social media, or television.

Fasting what has the most control over your life allows God into that space. Pray for the Holy Spirit's guidance on what to fast, when to fast, and how long. If you have something in your life that you jokingly say, "Oh, I could never survive a day without ...", then that might just be the place to start. Be intentional by journaling your prayer requests before you start and then document the truths God shows you along the way.

I started a 40-day fast, praying for God to move into the life of my 18-year-old son, in October 2019. In late January 2020, God answered with a holy transformation ... it was MASSIVE! God has answered literally all of my prayer requests lifted to Him during periods of fasting and prayer; well, all but one.... and that one, while not yet completed, was reconfirmed.

Remember, there is no secret formula to prayer and fasting. It is simply a desire to surrender and allow God to become your sole (and soul) source of survival and sustenance rather than the thing or activity that occupies your time or focus. During my journey, the most significant blessing and tool for waiting well has come from the power in prayer and fasting. Don't miss out on this incredible blessing from God.

FASTING IS A MEANS OF REPENTANCE:

> *And the people of Nineveh believed God. They called for a fast and put on sackcloth, from the greatest of them to the least of them. When God saw what they did, how they turned from their evil way, God relented of the disaster he had said he would do to them, and he did not do it.*
>
> — JONAH 3:5, 3:10 ESV

FASTING IS A MEANS OF SEEKING DIRECTION, CLARITY, AND PURPOSE:

> *As they were worshiping the Lord and fasting, the Holy Spirit said, "Set apart for me Barnabas and Saul for the work to which I have called them.*
>
> — ACTS 13:2

Fasting is a means of spiritual warfare:

Isn't this the fast I choose: To break the chains of wickedness, to untie the ropes of the yoke, to set the oppressed free, and to tear off every yoke?

— ISAIAH 58:6

Fasting is a means of replacing the world's influence with Jesus' presence:

Jesus said to them, "I am the Bread of Life. Come every day to me and you will never be hungry. Believe in me and you will never be thirsty."

— JOHN 6:35 TPT

But if anyone drinks the living water I give them, they will never thirst again and will be forever satisfied. For when you drink the water I give you, it becomes a gushing fountain of the Holy Spirit, springing up and flooding you with endless life!

— JOHN 4:14 TPT

REFLECTION QUESTIONS:

1. Is fasting a regular part of your faith walk with the Lord? If not, what has kept you from stepping into this type of submission?
2. Is there something in your life you "can't live without"?

PRAYER PAUSE:

Lord, you know better than anyone the importance and difficulty of fasting. As I prepare to fast _____, help me to draw strength and endurance from you and your Word. I want to know you as the Bread of Life and my Living Water. Thank you for being my ultimate provision and satisfaction. As I fast, draw me close and let your presence be tangible to me. More of you and less of me. In Jesus' name. Amen.

KELLY L. MURPHY

KING JEHOSHAPHAT, PAUL AND SILAS

DAY 21

Sometimes we find ourselves in battles over situations that we are powerless to change on our own. Have you become discouraged and started believing change would never happen? Have you prayed and fasted but then gave up? 2 Chronicles 20:1-30 is our story!!!

Just like King Jehoshaphat and his people in that time, we are powerless to see this battle to success; we know it is in God's hands. Like them, we look to you, God, for clarity and direction. You are truly the ONLY one who can deliver.

> *"Jehoshaphat was afraid, and he resolved to seek the Lord. Then he proclaimed a fast for all Judah, who gathered to seek the Lord. They even came from all the cities of Judah to seek Him."*
>
> — 2 CHRONICLES 20:3-4

> *God declared, "Do not be afraid. Do not be discouraged, for the battle is not yours, but God's. You do not have to fight this battle. Position yourselves, stand still, and see the salvation of the Lord. He is with you. Do not be afraid or discouraged. Tomorrow go out to face them for the Lord is with you."*
>
> — 2 CHRONICLES 20:15-17

In that story, the people humbled themselves, falling down before the Lord in worship. When they arose, their faith and trust were so strong that they assigned people to sing and praise God, AHEAD of their armed forces. Picture that ... the WORSHIP TEAM led the way before the army walking towards the battlefield!! Giving glory to God preceded all else. Their trust and faith in God's directives were greater than any fear of defeat. The moment, THE MOMENT, they began their shouts of praise and singing God delivered the victory!!!

Now turn to the New Testament, Acts 16:25. Paul and Silas had just been publicly beaten for witnessing about Jesus. They were stripped of clothes and hit with rods across their backs. Bloody and literally beaten down, they were thrown into a prison cell in the innermost area of the prison, which meant highest security, complete darkness, maximum confinement, and shackles on their feet. At this moment, when they had every physical reason to be angry at God, to doubt their calling, to question if it was really worth all the effort (you know, all those mental games that spin out of control when we feel under siege) ... when all these thoughts could have plagued their minds, Paul and Silas made a conscious decision to choose praise, to worship God.

They started singing songs that celebrated the greatness of God, loud enough for all the others prisoners to hear. In the utter darkness, there was no despair, because they worshipped God's goodness in the midst of their own suffering. I've read this before and focused my attention only on their choice to worship, which truly is amazing. But I missed the fact that "all the other prisoners listened to their worship." These other prisoners were in darkness as well, but they could hear the joy and peace through these two people, who had absolutely nothing physical to be joyful about.

In the midst of praying and praising, God shook the prison with a powerful earthquake, immediately opening all the doors and freeing all the shackles. We know it was God. After all, only God provides an earthquake strong enough to shake open prison doors and break chains, but doesn't crumble the actual building!

The prisoners didn't rush out, fearing the earthquake or escaping for their own freedom. They stayed right where the praise and worship were happening! How many of us would stick around in our prisons if we could escape? And then, the prison guard was about to end his own life, thinking the prisoners had escaped and would come after him, or worse, his superiors would kill him.

> *But Paul shouted in the darkness, "Stop! Don't hurt yourself! We're all still here."*
>
> — ACTS 16:28

How did Paul know the prison guard was going to attempt suicide if it was completely dark? God knew!

> *The jailer called for a light and he saw they were still in their cells. He rushed in and fell trembling at their feet and he brought them outside. He asked, "What must I do to be saved?*
>
> — ACTS 16:19-20

God used Paul and Silas' pain, their darkness, their chains to bring those around them to God's freedom. The prisoners, the guard, and his family all had their lives radically changed that day because of the pain experienced by two men obedient to God. When the enemy thought physical pain, imprisonment, and utter darkness would end the message, God broke through it all. Paul and Silas never took their eyes off God, even in their weakness, because they had God's strength to lean into. Not a minute of their situation, their pain, or the suffering was wasted.

God continually reminds us that this victory, the one looming on the other side of the mountain, is not one we will battle. And that's why we need to remember these stories ... why we need to avoid discouragement. Never did King Jehoshaphat or Paul and Silas say, "I give up", "this is never going to change," or "I doubt if God wants to even do this". While I may feel powerless in my situation, I need to remember my actions of thanking God, praying and singing to God all hold the power to break through any prison, any battle, any anything.

We are encouraged to pray, thank, sing, worship, and praise Him BEFORE the breakthrough is ever seen on the horizon. He wants our faith to drive our actions versus any proof in front of us. When we want to escape the stress and pressure of life and times that feel like imprisonment, we need to stop and realize there's earth shaking power in that prison. God shows up in the prison and wants to set us free.

REFLECTION QUESTIONS:

1. How do the stories in 2 Chronicles 20 and Acts 16 correlate to your own situation? How can you adjust your approach to worship and praise God in the midst of your pain, crisis, and turmoil?
2. When those moments of giving up overwhelm you, how can you act differently to be more like Paul, Silas, and King Jehoshaphat?

PRAYER PAUSE:

Lord, I admit that I have been more like the jailer than Paul and Silas. But right now, I am asking you to help adjust my approach to worship and praise. Amid pain, crisis, and turmoil, help my knees hit the floor and my hands be lifted towards Heaven before I attempt to do anything in my own strength. You move Heaven and Earth through praise and worship, and I want to be a part of it. Thank you for showing up in my prisons and setting me free. It is in your name, Jesus, that I pray. Amen.

WAITING WELL CHANGES EVERYTHING

RESIST THE URGE TO GO FISHING!

DAY 22

Sarah and Abraham were given a promise from God, one that would birth many nations, but Sarah grew weary and very impatient waiting for God to deliver. She watched days and months pass with no change, no baby growing inside her. She watched years pass by as she and her husband grew older, and the promise from God was more distant and unlikely.

Eventually, the all-consuming need to satisfy her inner longings and insecurities elevated to the danger zone. No doubt the enemy was right there in those moments to launch fiery darts of doubt into her mind:

Did God *really* give Abraham that promise?

Did God change His mind?

Did I do something wrong because it's taking so long?

What if I just did *this* for a faster result?

Sarah's solution was,

> *Since the Lord has prevented me from bearing children, go to my slave; perhaps through her I can build a family.*
>
> — GENESIS 16:2

Can you hear Sarah's desperation in the conversation with her husband? Unfortunately, Abraham agreed to Sarah's idea, even though He was the one who received the covenant promise from God.

We've all been there. Those early days of waiting can be quite an emotional wrestling match. You want to see that God is moving, to know that He is working in your situation. You want human reassurance that there's still a chance; there's still love or hope; you want connection and communication in this barren, quiet season. You really just want a moment of reprieve from pain and rejection.

I plead with you. Do NOT manipulate situations to gain outcomes sought by your emotions. Do not go fishing for compliments, for reassurances, for anything attached to your insecurities. These fishing expeditions to see if God is making good on His promises are baited by hooks of distrust, doubt, fear, and anxiety. Nothing good comes out of the pursuit of soothing insecurities, especially when those desired reassurances are to come from someone in your life with a heart that is not in alignment with God. Fishing for the things you want and manipulating circumstances before the timing of God to give them will only snag you a big ole stump at the bottom of a slow-moving, muddy river.

Setting up conversations to hear and orchestrate what you want may sound enticing and productive in the short-term, but it opens a long-term connection to the enemy that you won't expect. Should you get what you seek, the enemy will then spend a lifetime casting doubt within your mind. *Would what I made happen have actually happened without my involvement?* That's a rabbit hole with no end and no peace.

After Sarah achieved the manipulation she sought, it didn't turn out like she wanted. She blamed Abraham, crying out,

> *You are responsible for my suffering!*
>
> — GENESIS 16:5

I imagine Sarah spent the rest of her days on earth second-guessing her choice, wondering if Hagar and her son would return one day (after Sarah's insecurities forced Abraham to send Hagar away) and claim more of what Sarah did not want her to have. All because Sarah didn't have the patience in her life to wait and let God move in the way He promised.

The choice to wait well is a daily surrender in faith, trusting that God is who He says and He will move in His own timing, not our timing. Release the need to see posts and statuses on social media. Let go of the urge to ask friends and family for nuggets of information and to manipulate conversations in order to hear what you want.

I love Genesis 21:1-2 ...

> *"The Lord came to Sarah as he had said and the Lord did for Sarah what he had promised. Sarah became pregnant and bore a son to Abraham in his old age (100 years!!), AT THE APPOINTED TIME God had told him." (emphasis added)*

After Sarah gave birth to Isaac, she said,

> *Who would have told Abraham that Sarah would nurse children? Yet I have borne a son for him in his old age.*
>
> — GENESIS 21: 7

Only God will turn those grueling seasons of waiting and persevering into seasons of transformation and celebration. Only God!

> *Behold, I am the Lord, the God of all flesh. Is there anything too hard for me?*
>
> — JEREMIAH 32:27

> *Truly I tell you, if anyone says to this mountain, "Be lifted up and thrown into the sea," and does not doubt in his heart, but believes that what he says will happen, it will be done for him.*

WAITING WELL CHANGES EVERYTHING

— MARK 11:23

REFLECTION QUESTIONS:

1. In what ways have you questioned God's desire to move in your situation? What types of doubtful words have infiltrated your mind?
2. Can you recall times when you went fishing for responses in order to calm your own internal insecurity? What ended up as the result of such casting out of your hook and bait?
3. What would you have said to Sarah over coffee when she shared her brainstorm?

_____
_____
_____
_____
_____
_____
_____
_____
_____
_____

WHEN GOD ORCHESTRATES A NEGATIVE TO GAIN A POSITIVE...

DAY 23

> *On this particular day, the Lord asked Satan, "Where have you come from?" "From roaming through the earth," Satan answered Him, "and walking around on it." Then the Lord said to Satan, "Have you considered my servant Job? No one else on earth is like him, a man of perfect integrity, who fears God and turns away from evil."*
>
> — JOB 1:7-8

We read in the second sentence of the first chapter that Job was a man of complete integrity who feared God and turned away from evil. By the third sentence, we are told Job was the greatest man among all the people of the east. And yet, God blatantly focused the enemy's attention directly on Job by asking, have you *considered* my servant?

> *Satan answered the Lord, "Does Job fear God for nothing? Haven't you placed a hedge around him, his household and everything he owns? You have blessed the work of his hands, and his possessions have increased in the land. But stretch out your hand and strike everything he owns, and he will surely curse you to your face." "Very Well," the Lord told Satan, "Everything he owns is in your power. However, do not lay a hand on Job himself." So Satan left the Lord's presence.*
>
> — JOB 1:9-12

I imagine Satan smugly sauntering off, thinking he was about to destroy another believer filled with an arrogance of power. While all along, God was orchestrating a negative action to produce a positive outcome.

We love to read that God parted the Red Sea. But no one wants to be backed into what feels like a painful dead end. We love to read that Job's life was far better in the second half of his years and that he gained far more materially than he had before all the devastation. But none of us wants to lose our families, our marriages, our homes, or lifestyles to gain the transformation and blessing God has for us.

Standing on a promise from God can feel as if we're walking in shifting sand, searching the horizon for any sense of relief, overwhelmed by the circumstances, while simultaneously riding a rollercoaster of anger, fear, doubt, and discouragement. But what if God has just orchestrated a negative to produce the positive, a divine set-up? Is it possible that the "thing" that has us so devastated right now has been allowed by God for a specific purpose? And, if that's the case, what are we to gain from it? How does God want to transform us?

Within these questions sits the blessing, the treasure. It's a perspective shift. In our own moments of tremendous pain and suffering, barriers and oppression, we ask God to show us what we are to learn and how we are to grow through the situation. We look at the dysfunction but lean into the reality that God wouldn't have us go through it all if He wasn't already in it, if He wasn't already with us every step of the way to make sure we get through it.

We can be comforted and assured that God creates guardrails containing and limiting the influence Satan is allowed in our lives, just as he did with Job. When God spoke to Satan, He limited the enemy's tactics. These boundaries reinforce for me that Satan never has free rein in my life, although he likes to boast as if he does, and I often relinquish power to him because of it. God allows only the precise amount of trial which will produce endurance, perseverance, and personal growth, transforming me to be more like Him. What's the precise amount? Well, I can't speak for you, but I often require far more heat to transform my personality, stubbornness, and pride into humility. I lean into the fact that what Satan intended to destroy me with God will use for my benefit and His glory.

I totally understand that this is no small task. When the enemy came to shred my home life, my faith wasn't anchored to navigate the storm. Through pain and tears, I turned inward to myself, to what would ease my pain. But now you better believe I seek the plan and purpose of God every time. I seek to find the divine setup, the holy treasure hunt that has made all the difference in those difficult seasons.

REFLECTIVE QUESTIONS:

1. As you consider this difficult season you're in, what can you gain from the circumstances?
2. In this same scenario, how do you think God wants to use it to transform you?
3. Our world says bad things shouldn't happen to good people. How do you think God will use the negatives surrounding your life to build your glorious testimony? Begin praying on that glorious testimony.

PRAYER PAUSE:

At the end of the Bible story, Job humbled himself before God. I come to you in this same humility, Lord.

"I know that you can do anything, and no plan of yours can be thwarted." v. 42:2

"Therefore, I reject my words and am sorry for them; I am dust and ashes." v. 42:6

"And as a result, the Lord blessed the last part of Job's life more than the first." v. 42:12

Holy Spirit, give me a new perspective to see the positives within the negatives. Guide me into greater transformation in your image through what the enemy has planned for evil against me. In Jesus' name, I pray. Amen.

WHEN WHAT YOU'VE BEEN PRAYING FOR JUST TOOK A DERAILMENT...

DAY 24

On a lazy Sunday evening, God's promise of restoration seemed to take a massive, unforeseen derailment. In the first few minutes of what could have been my emotional train wreck, the most surreal calmness gently moved through me, defying the meltdown my flesh so eagerly craved. God was in those moments, bringing me peace and ironically reinforcing that nothing had changed, even when my eyes testified everything had changed.

God reinforced that my future days of worshipping Him, praying to Him and anchoring my hope and faith on His promise of restoration and reconciliation were to continue just as strongly as they had in the days prior to those chaotic moments. The message was clear: *JUST AS I HAD DONE BEFORE I WAS TO CONTINUE.*

But how do I know *for sure* that this was a directive from God? While my eyes were closed in prayer, the fan blew the weightless pages of my Bible, by no coincidence resting open at Daniel 6.

I knew Daniel was a pillar of faith, obediently and faithfully serving the Lord, but I sensed the Holy Spirit wanted me to focus on what happened when a significant barrier was placed in front of him. Did Daniel cry out, I can't do this anymore? Did he weaken to the pressures of the king, his co-workers, and the world? Did he forego God's spiritual truths for what could only be seen as the world's truths being played out in front of him?

The edict had been signed by King Darius, stating no worshipping or petitioning of any god or man, other than to worship the king himself for 30 days. Scripture says,

> *"WHEN Daniel learned that the document had been signed, he went into his house."*
>
> — DANIEL 6:10A

Don't miss this critical detail! Before God stepped into Daniel's circumstances, Daniel stepped out in tremendous obedience, not to man, but to God.

> "The windows in Daniel's upstairs room opened toward Jerusalem. Three times a day he got down on his knees, prayed and gave thanks to God, JUST AS HE HAD DONE BEFORE." *(add emphasis)*
>
> — DANIEL 6:10B

The enemy manipulated people and circumstances, purposed to stop Daniel's daily communications with God, but those barriers would not derail Daniel's obedience, even if that obedience meant losing his life. Daniel prayed and gave thanks despite what had been declared by the edict. This point, right here, is where we often face the greatest struggle with our faith. We allow the circumstances and what we see to affect our submission to God.

Daniel was obedient. He loved and served God. The king's edict would not divert that obedience. As a result, judgement and punishment of death by the lion's den were delivered upon Daniel. How many times have you prayed, and the situation worsened? How many times have you obediently served at church, tithed, fasted, and prayed, yet the circumstances didn't change? God uses those darkest moments to bring about His greatest glory in your life.

> *After rolling a stone barrier in front of the entrance to the lions' den, which trapped Daniel inside, the king placed a seal on the stone with the signet rings of him and his nobles, indicating that nothing in regard to Daniel could be changed.*
>
> — DANIEL 6:17

Isn't that just like our arrogant and prideful ways? Man makes his plans, looks at the outward circumstances, and foolishly believes that his final say is actually THE final say. While one person deems their action or decision as a done deal, a follower of Jesus stands in obedience, faith, and trust in God, demonstrating that anything can be radically transformed. No stone is permanent. No promise of God will go unanswered.

> *At first light of dawn, the king got up and hurried to the lions' den. When he reached the den, he cried out in anguish to Daniel. "Daniel, servant of the living God," the king said, "has your God, whom you continually serve, been able to rescue from the lions?" Then Daniel spoke with the king: "May the king live forever. My God sent his angel and shut the lions' mouths; and they haven't harmed me, for I was found innocent before Him. And also before you, Your Majesty. I have not done harm." The king was overjoyed and gave orders to take Daniel out of the den. Then King Darius wrote to those of every people, nation, and language who live on the whole earth: "May your prosperity abound. I have issued a decree that in all my royal dominion, people must tremble in fear before the God of Daniel: For his is the living God, and he endures forever; his kingdom will never be destroyed, and his dominion has no end. He rescues and delivers; he performs signs and wonders in the heavens and on earth, for he has rescued Daniel from the power of the lions."*
>
> — DANIEL 6:19-27

Daniel's ordeal became a glorious testimony for King Darius and all in the kingdom to witness God's faithfulness and provision. What God did for Daniel is not unique; He will do it for you, too. When the unexpected takes you by surprise, be obedient, be filled with hope and thanksgiving, and be ready to hear from the Lord. Don't let the circumstances deter you, disrupt your faith, or distract you from your focus on God. Bow low to your knees in those moments of chaos and uncertainty. Praise Him. Worship Him. And in obedience, DO JUST AS YOU HAD DONE BEFORE. Then watch as God shuts the mouths of the lions in your life.

> *Behold, I give unto you power to tread on serpents and scorpions, and over all the power of the enemy: and nothing shall by any means hurt you.*
>
> — LUKE 10:19 KJV

REFLECTIVE QUESTIONS:

1. In those moments when your situation has appeared impossible, what's been your typical reaction? How could you step into a Daniel-type reaction?
2. As you're praying for the situation to change, imagine a glorious testimony. Who around you would gain from witnessing God's glory on display, like King Darius? Make a list of those people and pray for their eyes to be opened as your answer to prayer comes about.
3. What has been declared a "done deal" in your life ... As if the power of God was not strong or able to change? Use

the authority given to you by Jesus to pray over that situation or person, as in Luke 10:19.

WAITING WELL CHANGES EVERYTHING

JONAH AND HIS SAILING COMPANIONS: PART ONE

DAY 25

AM I A SAILOR ON JONAH'S BOAT?

When Jonah defied God's instructions and boarded the ship, the hearts of the sailors were separated from God. When turmoil arrived, they unsuccessfully prayed to their (little-g) gods; but, by the end-of-chapter one,

> *The men were seized by great fear of the Lord, and they offered a sacrifice to the Lord and made vows.*
>
> —JONAH 1:16

These sailors were worshipping the world's gods, but when calamity struck and fear seized their minds, it was to the Lord upon which they turned. This scripture highlights two important messages not to be overlooked:

1. God will use the struggles of the person you are praying for to minister to you and others in ways you won't anticipate. While Jonah was still acting in disobedience, God was bringing glory and testimony in the purposed storm. He reached the sailors hearts despite the disobedience of Jonah turning away from God. The Lord wanted all the sailors to seek Him, so He used that one storm to turn the hearts of all involved, even before Jonah repented.
2. While the one you pray for may be a lot like Jonah, it's important that we, the praying ones, aren't like the sailors on the boat ... rowing, rowing, rowing to shore, in their own strength and determination. Did you notice the storm intensified, and the sailors were *"seized by a great fear"* rather than listening to what Jonah had to say? When the sailors abandoned their plans of frantically rowing to shore in their own strength and followed the direction, the sea stopped raging. Once they surrendered and became obedient to God's direction, and the sea calmed, scripture noted a change within them ... *"they offered a sacrifice to the Lord and made vows."*

I am often like those sailors ... doing everything in my strength and my wisdom, thinking it's my duty to get the one I want to help through the storm and to dry land. I often succumb to the surrounding circumstances, resulting in fear and anxiety rather than allowing respect and reverence of the Lord to guide my reactions and calm the storm.

There's no doubt that God wants us involved in His rescue mission of souls. But the way we conduct ourselves within God's plans could intensify the raging storm that is surrounding the person we're praying for. It's not my role to calm their storm, to fix their chaos, to interfere in the plans God has to reach them. Yes, it's hard to watch a storm brew; and often, we will experience collateral damage in that storm.

That's why we should be anchored securely to scripture and steadfastly standing on the shore, ready and willing to assist, when and ONLY when, God says it's time. Calm those fears that perpetuate you trying to control the situation or wanting to know what's going on in the life of a disobedient "Jonah". God knows far more than you, orchestrating details you can't fathom or think about. His ways are not our ways ... and thank God for THAT!

REFLECTIVE QUESTIONS:

1. In what ways have you tried to step in and "help" God with the rescue of a Jonah-type person? Can you say the actions you've taken have been God-ordained or based upon your own assessment of the situation?
2. Learning to wait well means trusting that God knows exactly when and how to orchestrate transformation. Is there a time when you stepped back and obediently allowed God to move in His timing? What were the fruits of that decision?

WAITING WELL CHANGES EVERYTHING

JONAH AND HIS SAILING COMPANIONS: PART TWO

DAY 26

A WALK IN THE OPPOSITE DIRECTION

When you receive guidance or instruction from the Lord, it doesn't mean you are required to follow the instructions, as we see in the story of Jonah. After he received instructions from God, Jonah intentionally boarded a ship that was heading into a vast ocean, traveling in the opposite direction of where those instructions should have taken him. Early in the voyage, Jonah stepped down to the lowest, darkest point on that ship to take a nap. His deep slumber then became a form of escape, a way to avoid and tune out the soul-stirring convictions of the Holy Spirit. Jonah 1:1-5.

When a person goes in the opposite direction from what God has called them to do, it's expected that they will hide — unconsciously or purposefully — just as Jonah did. It's not likely that a person will board a literal ship and take a nap, but you may see them display behaviors of avoidance, like moving out of photos that place them with people, or in locations and situations that could hold them accountable for their actions. They may withdraw from social media to limit others' access to information. They filter stories, remove details, and censor information. Shifting sands of truth may mark their interactions. Even their choice of words will adjust, talking in the first person of "I" in all their discussions to avoid placing them with people, avoiding the use of names to create distance. They minimize contact and involvement with those who know of God's instructions for their life or will encourage their faith. They will increase contact with those who are not likely to hold them accountable but will provide sought-after distractions from the truth.

Are you watching and absorbing these behaviors as personal affronts or attacks? Are you interpreting these actions as rejections of you? It's critical to understand that these activities are centered around the person's own walk with God. It's their own internal processing of convictions between them and the Holy Spirit.

Jonah didn't stop being a messenger of God for the people of Nineveh because of his hiding and fleeing. God orchestrated the circumstances around Jonah to bring him back into alignment and obedience with what God was commanding him to do. God allowed time for the process to unfold and the chiseling of Jonah's character. Often the plans a person makes apart from God will become a train wreck ... or ... the person gets everything they seek, only to realize everything they asked for is meaningless and brings them no contentment. Learning the truth that independence from God is void of true and lasting peace, joy, and contentment is often a lengthy time-stealing ordeal, both for the one learning and the one praying.

When you're the one watching someone turn away from God and go their own way, there's a process occurring within you as well. The patience and fortitude to stand in the gap of faith and pray without ceasing will build endurance and perseverance. But it should also build patience and empathy to realize it's not all about what you've been told will come to pass. God was patiently waiting for Jonah to choose an alignment of the heart under HIS perfect plan and purpose. He was waiting for Jonah to surrender his own will for God's will. If God was doing all that waiting for Jonah, why should we be exempt from waiting?

Fleeing from God's directive and plan/purpose is serious business. But don't think for a second that once a person has traveled down the road of disobedience, it's over. God never left Jonah, nor abandoned him because of his choices. He's not going to leave you, nor will He abandon the one in your life who is hiding for a season. Prayer is a powerful weapon in the hands of those who choose to use it.

Your Sheep.

Your Plan

Your Rescue.

Your Timing.

All for Your Glory, God.

REFLECTIVE QUESTIONS:

1. Are there hurtful behaviors that you're processing as personal attacks towards you? If they are symptoms of a person's disobedience to what God is calling in their life, how can you change your reactions? How can you be a window through which they can see Jesus in your actions?
2. In what ways can you see the life of Jonah playing out in your loved one? Can you read the book of Jonah and see how God is all about second chances, for Jonah, the sailors and the citizens of Nineveh?

PRAYER PAUSE:

God, please stir a deep and mighty discontentment, dissatisfaction, and distaste in their heart for everything that is not YOUR best in their lives. Give them strength and conviction to step into the Holy Spirit's whisper, calling for their attention. Alter those circumstances to apply just the right amount of pressure for them to turn their heads upwards to you, to change their posture to one of surrender and obedience to you, alone.

And then do the same for me.

_____

_____

_____

_____

WAITING WELL CHANGES EVERYTHING

KELLY L. MURPHY

HAPPY TIMES DON'T BUILD ENDURANCE AND PERSEVERANCE

DAY 27

There has never been a single happy time that ever contributed to building endurance and perseverance in my faith. Happy times do not require a rugged commitment to stay the course or teach us to anchor and align our hearts under God's authority for the future storms and chaos. It's the gut wrenching, tears flowing, fervently praying times of waiting on God that build endurance and perseverance. Great transformation happens in those exhaustive moments of not seeing a shred of evidence on the horizon, but we continue to walk in faith and trust that God will move in His timing.

Let's be honest ... standing obediently on a promise from God has some pretty rough moments. It is often exhaustive, hard, emotion-crushing work. Even "being still" is work for someone, like me, who lives their life in constant motion. However, the resulting transformation is also the most amazing rise from the ashes that you will ever experience this side of heaven ... when you choose to allow it to change you for the better.

Transformation is a choice. You can choose to take a seat in the same spot where it all fell apart, or you can choose to move forward into allowing God to make all things new, including you. Remember, transformation and restoration are not destinations. We don't arrive and proudly say, "Here I am! Done and transformed!!" It's a gradual process refined by the fires of standing and waiting.

My choice to step into transformation occurred in October 2018. I was two years into this standing journey. I remember an incredible boldness overcoming me during a conversation with my husband, as I stated, "This is the deal. We are at a 'Y' in the road. We are both standing at this point right here, right now. You can go to the left and go your own way but know that I am going to the right. I am chasing hard after God. I will follow Him, surrender to Him and be obedient to Him. I'm all done with the emotional back and forth. I'm all done with a surface level faith. You've told me God showed you what He intends for us. I want you to go with me on this journey, but know that when we leave this moment, the decision for me has already been made. I will never cease praying for you, but I'm all done persuading you."

That was my line in the sand, my stake in the ground, my choice, and my declaration. God would reign over all else in my life. Never did I anticipate or realize what a game changer that one choice, that one declaration, would be for me. While the journey to restoration and waiting upon God's promise always felt like watching honey crawl out of a bottle, the transformation within me has been like

God's wide-open faucet beautifully and abundantly filling me with His Living Water.

Please don't miss this point ... God is looking for you to boldly choose Him. It won't be easy. And yeah, it's going to be crushingly hard. But we serve a faithful God that will never abandon us. In my half-century of life, this one choice has turned out to be the best, most radical, life affirming choice.

If you haven't already, I urge you to take your eyes off the dysfunction currently spinning around you and proclaim your choice to chase hard after God. Radically and fully, choose God now during your pain and suffering, and then watch as His Living Word manifests in your life. We can come to God by choice and enjoy immense blessings or we can come to Him as a final, last resort. It's all a choice.

> *And not only that, but we also boast in our afflictions, because we know that affliction produces endurance, endurance produces proven character, and proven character produces hope. This hope will not disappoint us, because God's love has been poured out in our hearts through the Holy Spirit who was given to us.*
>
> — ROMANS 5:3-5

PRAYER PAUSE:

Have you boldly chosen to walk in the ways of the Lord? What is your personal declaration? If you haven't yet, I urge you to write it out on paper ... state it clearly and boldly. Declare your intentions to the Lord. And then pray for the Holy Spirit to open your eyes to ways of walking out that declaration. Pray for people to be placed in your path both to help and to be blessed by. Pray for the Bible to come to life in ways that direct you. And above all, simply abide in the unconditional love God has for you.

WAITING WELL CHANGES EVERYTHING

DREAMS, SIGNS AND REINFORCEMENTS

DAY 28

God's chosen people were CHOSEN. God actually placed His glorious favor upon them. They repeatedly saw nourishment fall from Heaven. They were rescued when a body of water parted in two. They claimed victories in battles and discernment for decisions when praying and fasting. And yet, after experiencing all those encounters with God and passing them on from generation to generation, they continually questioned and doubted God's presence and goodness. The grass seemed so much greener in the yards of those who were "unchosen". The Israelites wanted to follow kings and worship tangible items they could see, like the rest of their neighbors. They looked to signs and reinforcements within the world rather than from God's Word.

If we don't allow the truth of scripture to overwhelm us and be planted deep within us, causing transformation through us, then our lives will become a desperate search for, and reliance upon, one sign after another, continually questioning and doubting, just like the Israelites.

What's the number on the clock say? What's the side of that truck say? Is it a sign? Could it be a sign? Ohhh, I hope it's a sign! How long does it take before the next bout of questioning takes root in your mind and that sign doesn't fill the void and cover the doubt within you? The search begins again with your eyes scanning the surrounding landscape. Just how many signs will actually calm the turmoil within you?

> *Then some of the scribes and Pharisees said to Him, "Teacher, we want to see a sign from you. He (Jesus) answered them, "An evil and adulterous generation demands a sign...."*
>
> — MATTHEW 12:38-39

During another occasion in Jesus' ministry, the same message was repeated,

> *"An evil and adulterous generation demands a sign, but no sign will be given to it except the sign of Jonah." Then he left them and went away.*
>
> — MATTHEW 16:4

Jesus clearly felt the need to reinforce this message, given He stated it more than once to more than one audience. What was the sign of Jonah? God gave Jonah a clear message to proclaim for the people of Nineveh, "In 40 days, Nineveh will be demolished!" Then the people of Nineveh believed God. Jonah 3:4-5.

In seven years of standing on a promise from God, I have received six significant messages of God's intended plan in my life. That's a ton of quiet hours in the journey of many, many waiting days. Interestingly enough, all of those signs arrived as blessings AFTER I stopped seeking them and after I began trusting God solely based upon who HE IS rather than what He provides as reassurances. I realized my obedience to God was being bartered in exchange for needing to see God move and reinforce His answer to prayer. This had to stop.

Today, I stand anchored on His many promises described throughout His Word. Literally, not figuratively, those scripture verses are my anchors. The messages and dreams He's given over these years are not the anchors; they are gifts, which add seasoning, color, and flavor to the journey.

What do I mean? Several years ago, God gave me a dream. I walked into this room of antiques, over to a large cabinet with glass shelves filled with the items you'd expect in an antique store. On the top shelf, layered in a light dust, was a circle where something was obviously taken because there was no dust, just the empty space. I instantly knew there was an old gold pocket watch, open like a clam shell, that had been sitting on this shelf. But in the dream it was missing, and I knew it was stolen. I then walked around a corner to another cabinet with glass shelves. On the top shelf was a velvet ring box, opened up with two gold wedding bands standing up in the slot. I stood staring at the ring box, wondering why such valuable jewelry was still there while the pocket watch was the only item gone. As I came out of the dream, I specifically asked the Holy Spirit what the dream meant. Immediately, I received a reply, "Time will be stolen, but I am protecting your relationship."

My faith in God's promise of restoration did not become anchored on that dream or any other of the six signs. My faith is anchored solely in His scriptures: 2 Corinthians 5:18; Numbers 23:19; 2 Chronicles 20:17; Psalms 9:9-10; Proverbs 3:5-6; Hebrews 13:5; Isaiah 13:5 and Philippians 4:7 ... and so many more additional promises.

This hard season of standing is a journey of transformation within you. God is using the wait to move you into a restored relationship with Him before He restores your relationship to someone else. Sometimes the journey will be blessed with signs along long stretches of quiet. Only God knows whether you have a reliance, dependence, and even idolatry upon seeing with your eyes or trusting Him with your faith. I urge you to seek the Holy Spirit's wisdom and discernment and be open to honestly addressing those areas to be shown.

> *Lord Jesus, I lift up the person reading this devotional right now and I ask you to open their mind to what you want to show them. Lord, this writing is not a sign or a message that they should anchor themselves to, but merely a means by which you provide color and support within their own journey. Give them wisdom and discernment to hear from the Holy Spirit so clearly that peace settles within their soul. Open up your Word in a way that brings fresh insight and rich blessings into their life. God, I ask you to bind up any evil influences that are aimed at distraction or dysfunction and are trying to divert focus*

away from your one true Savior, Jesus. It's in His name, I pray. Amen.

REFLECTIVE QUESTIONS:

1. Do you often find yourself scanning the horizon for signs and messages in times of weakness and insecurity? Consider creating a small pocket-sized list of scriptures that can be accessed in these times.
2. As you look back over this journey, what are the messages and moments of color and flavor given to you by the Holy Spirit as blessings in your life?

PRAYER PAUSE:

Lord, forgive me for all the times I looked for signs instead of seeking you. Signs don't save, heal, or fix anything. Only you can. Change my heart so that you are its one true desire. In your name, Jesus, I bind up any evil influences that are aimed at distraction or disfunction and are trying to divert my focus away from you. Help me to have wisdom and discernment so that I may hear clearly from the Holy Spirit and internalize your Word. It is in your name, Jesus, that I pray. Amen.

BINDING UP AND FILLING UP

DAY 29

Spiritual warfare ... it scares many Christians into avoidance. But actually, it's one of the most detailed topics in the Bible. God wants us poised and prepared; He wants us knowledgeable and keenly ready for the schemes of the enemy. And He's provided everything we need to know within the pages of scripture.

His Word states that when we command "In Jesus' name," evil spirits will flee. Before we bind up and cast out in spiritual warfare, and before we come before the Lord with any such request, it is imperative to first take time to repent. Humbly go before the Lord and seek forgiveness of any places where sin may have taken hold in yourself. Imagine a rain gutter clogged with the debris of disappointment, anger, bitterness, doubt, and discouragement. God's Living Water can't flow through that vessel freely and powerfully until all that debris is cleaned out. Once the impediments are removed, prayers and the Holy Spirit can flow freely and effectively.

During a time in the Synagogue, Jesus was handed the scroll of Isaiah. After finding a specific place in the scripture, He read it out loud to those in His presence:

> *The Spirit of the Lord is on me, because he has anointed me to preach good news to the poor. He has sent me to proclaim release to the captives and recovery of sight to the blind, to set free the oppressed, to proclaim the year of the Lord's favor.*
>
> — LUKE 4:18-19 CSB

Jesus told the Disciples that they would do even greater things through HIS name after He departed. Read Luke 4:18-19 again. Believe in the authority Jesus has given to us through the power of His name, crucifixion, and resurrection. The binding and removal of evil spirits happens because we have taken the time to repent of our own sins, aligned our hearts under God, and called upon the AUTHORITY that is activated through Jesus' name. Do not be deceived by the enemy; it is not authority or power we own, but what is only accessible through Jesus.

It is CRITICAL to conclude with prayer, seeking an immediate filling of that newly created void of space. Pray for an indwelling of the Holy Spirit and God's truth, love, mercy, and grace to occupy what has just been emptied of evil spirits. Do NOT leave that space void. If it's a physical space, pray that the Holy Spirit will take up residence and bless all who enter. If it's a person you've just prayed over, it's important for them to come in agreement with you as you pray together for Jesus' presence to become the sole authority in their life.

Why do we do this? Jesus specifically warned us in Luke 11:24-26 and in Matthew 12:43-45:

> *When an unclean spirit comes out of a person, it roams through waterless places looking for rest but doesn't find any. Then it says, 'I'll go back to my house that I came from.' Returning, it finds the house vacant, swept, and put in order. Then it goes and brings with it seven other spirits more evil than itself, and they enter and settle down there. As a result, that person's last condition is worse than the first. That's how it will also be with this evil generation.*

So what does that look like when praying? Lord, I ask you to place Godly men and women in _____'s path to speak truth into their life and help guide them to you. Bind up every evil spirit that seeks to kill, steal, destroy, manipulate, and condemn, through the blood of Jesus' crucifixion and the power of Jesus' name. Cast those spirits where you so choose, Jesus. In the void from the binding up of those spirits, place an overwhelming and sudden longing in their heart for you. Holy Spirit, fill them with Living Water and your presence. Plant seeds of love, grace, and mercy, and open their eyes to the salvation found only in you, Jesus. Convict their heart of past sins and guide them through full reconciliation with you. It's in JESUS' name that I pray, Amen.

During this time of prayer, you may want to anoint the space or the person with oil as well. Anointing oil is Biblical in its practice, setting apart those acting on God's behalf, to consecrate the tabernacle, to heal the sick, and to usher in the Holy Spirit in alignment with God's truth and love. While there was a specific mixture of fine spices with oil used by Moses in Exodus 30:32-33, as well as prophets and the Disciples, the use of pure virgin olive oil works too.

What does that look like? Before praying over the purest olive oil in my home, I repented and prayed on the armor of Ephesians 6. Having an empty "vessel" within myself, I then poured a small amount of the oil into the glass vial and prayed:

> *In Jesus' name, I lift up this oil, dedicating and consecrating it to You and Your Kingdom. Lord, I ask You to release the power of Your blood over this oil and sanctify it. Your blood breaks all curses and demonic assignments, cleanses and destroys all darkness. Through the blood of Jesus, I declare this anointing oil is now redeemed out of the hand of the devil and into the hands of God, set apart for the plans and purposes of God, for the Glory of God by the Blood of Jesus. God, I ask You to bless this oil and pour Your Holy Spirit upon and into this oil. In Jesus' name I proclaim that Your Holy Spirit is now activated upon this oil and every place it is poured, applied, everywhere it touches and passes near shall release the Power of Your Holy Spirit. In Jesus' name, I call this oil blessed, holy, sanctified, and set apart to be used only for the Kingdom and the Glory of God, in Jesus' name, Amen!*

— AUTHOR UNKNOWN

With the blessed oil, I then anoint the person or place. For example, I walk around our home creating a small sign of the cross over the entryways, bedrooms, and any areas where the enemy seeks entry, such as computers, televisions, phones, etc. I can testify that the atmosphere in our home shifts radically. Anointing is like praying and fasting; it is never a "one and done" action. We can be in a space or place of closeness to God, only to then open ourselves unintentionally to influences of the enemy. I know with great certainty that our home always feels like a refuge from the world because of the regular anointing by the Holy Spirit.

One final note of awareness. There are several locations (1 Samuel, Judges 9; 2 Chronicles 18; 1 Kings 22) in the Old Testament when "The Lord sent an evil spirit ..." I encourage you to read them and understand the details of why God commanded them. While the enemy seeks bondage over all of us, remember that God has the ultimate and final authority. After you repent, but <u>before</u> you seek to bind up and cast out evil spirits, be sure to pray for God's wisdom and guidance. While your prayers and anointing will not remove an evil spirit sent by God, it is always a good practice to seek His direction and confirmation that the place you are standing is where God wants you to be. In my earlier days of Christ-following, I wrongly assumed presence in battles God did not call me to fight. Your greatest, most effective, and efficient victories will always come after you repent, seek confirmation from God, and then armor up before stepping into HIS battlefield.

_____

_____

_____

THE POWER OF WORDS

DAY 30

Just how powerful are the words spoken into our lives? Adam and Eve were living their best life in the garden. They were communing with God and enjoying all He created. Then the enemy arrived on the scene with a prompting still in use today: "Did God REALLY say ...?"

First, a little backstory: Eve had yet to be created when God instructed Adam not to touch the tree, but she eventually received the directive from Adam. She never questioned what God had told Adam about the forbidden tree. Even scripture's notation of the tree's location in the garden is interesting:

> *The Lord God caused to grow out of the ground every tree pleasing in appearance and good for food, including the tree of life in the MIDDLE of the*

> *garden, as well as the tree of the knowledge of good and evil. (emphasis added)*
>
> — GENESIS 2:9 CSB

This forbidden tree was planted in the middle of the garden, which meant Adam and Eve walked by it frequently. Think about it ... if something is in the middle of your daily environment, then it's unavoidable and becomes commonplace to your surroundings.

But then along came Satan with his strategically simple question,

> *Has God really said, "You shall not eat from ANY tree of the garden"?*
>
> — GENESIS 3:1

Eve innocently engaged in the conversation, unaware of the enemy's ultimate goal of influencing her thinking.

> *And when the woman SAW that the tree was good for food, and that it was pleasant to the eyes, and a tree to be desired to make one wise, she took of the fruit...*
>
> — GENESIS 3:6 KJV

The emphasis in that scripture is mine. Don't miss the modest little "saw" in that verse. The fruit of the tree didn't suddenly change its form. It didn't go from being drab, dull, and unnoticeable yesterday to being vivid, eye-catching, and desirable to her the next day. It was the same tree producing the same fruit, which she and Adam had walked by and viewed every single day.

So what happened? What changed? The power of words changed how truth was perceived.

Words were spoken. In a brief moment of conversation with an outside influence, those few words transformed how Eve perceived the same truth that was always in front of her. Her viewpoint changed, and then her choices changed.

When you're standing on a promise from God, outside influences will come. It's guaranteed. Those voices may be whispers in your mind from the enemy or it could even be from well-intentioned Christians. But the internal churning within your mind is still the same: "Did God really tell me to stand or am I just doing it because I want it?" "Does God really even want to answer my prayer?"

There are so many versions of the enemy's "Did God really say ..." but they are all designed for one specific purpose–for you to doubt God. The enemy's mission is to distort, distract and discourage your stand and, ultimately, your faith, by using anyone and anything as influences.

The words you allow to infiltrate your mind can drastically impact your stand. What words spoken to you today have altered your view or stand from yesterday? Are you seeing a situation in front of you and judging it based on the thoughts being whispered into your mind or spoken by those around you?

Or are you walking a 2 Corinthians 10:5 mindset?

> *We demolish arguments and every pretention that sets itself up against the knowledge of God, and we take captive every though to make it obedient to Christ.*
>
> — 2 CORINTHIANS 10:5 NIV

We don't wake up one day and find God's Word suddenly different. His Word is the same today as it was yesterday and as it will be tomorrow. Waiting well means being confidently anchored to the rock of His Word, even amid shifting sands, prolonged wilderness seasons, and the words of those around us.

REFLECTIVE QUESTIONS:

1. What specific words have been spoken to you that caused you to pause and question your stand? Are you giving more power to those words than scripture?
2. How will you intentionally "take captive" the words spoken over you that contradict what God says about you or a situation?
3. When the enemy speaks lies, hold fast to God's truth with scripture. Taking thoughts captive means covering them or shutting them down with what God says is the truth. Look up and write out these contradictions on sticky notes for posting where you need the reminders:

When the enemy says you've lost the battle, Romans 8:37 says...

When the enemy says to be fearful, 2 Timothy 1:7 says...

When the enemy says God isn't listening, Psalms 34:17 says...

When the enemy says you'll never be healed, Psalms 147:3 says...

When the enemy says it will never change, Isaiah 43:18-19 says...

When the enemy says it's hopeless, Jeremiah 29:11 says...

When the enemy says it's impossible, Matthew 19:26 says...

PRAYER PAUSE:

So many times, we pray God will CONFIRM what we are thinking, give us a sign that we are okay to do what we want, or approve a decision we've technically already made.

What we should actually pray for is the Holy Spirit to CONFORM our thoughts in alignment to God's plan. We are called to obey, surrendering our will to God's authority over us. This posture is difficult but very rewarding, even through the most difficult of times.

WAITING WELL CHANGES EVERYTHING

RELEASING HOW WE THINK IT SHOULD ALL GO

DAY 31

In 2 Kings 5, we are told that Naaman, the army's commander, had won many battles in his professional life. Now, he faced a personal battle with a skin disease that was void of victory. His wife's servant suggested Naaman should go see a man in Israel who could cure him.

With gold, silver, and clothing as payment, Naaman traveled to purchase his skin cure from the king of Israel. Elisha, God's prophet, heard of Naaman's plight and sent a messenger to him with very specific instructions.

> *"Tell him to go wash seven times in the Jordan River and your skin will be restored and you will be clean."*
>
> — 2 KINGS 5:10

Go, Naaman, move. You take the step first.

Wash seven times...not once or twice, but seven times; obey the duration of the instructions, Naaman.

In the Jordan; go exactly where I tell you to go, not where you think you should go or where others have had success.

Your skin will be restored, and you will be clean. It was through obedience to complete the stated steps that resulted in total restoration.

Now here is where we can often act just like Naaman:

> *But Naaman got angry and left, saying, 'I was telling myself: He will surely come out, stand and call on the name of the Lord his God, and wave his hand over the place and cure the skin disease. Aren't Abana and Pharpar, the rivers of Damascus, better than all the waters of Israel? Couldn't I wash in them and be clean?' So he turned and left in a rage.*
>
> — 2 KINGS 5:11-12

Naaman became frustrated and angry and walked away from his potential restoration. Why? Because Naaman expected Elisha, as God's prophet, to address him, not through a communication from his messenger. Because Naaman expected Elisha to do the healing himself, by actions Naaman thought were more appropriate. And because the instructions weren't happening in the way, the place, and the manner Naaman wanted.

WAITING WELL CHANGES EVERYTHING

Naaman wanted the blessing but only in the way he perceived and judged that it should happen.

His own heart was not yet in a position of alignment to receive the blessing of restoration God had for him. Naaman's traveling companions provided him with truth and were able to shed light on Naaman's prideful attitude.

> *But his servants approached and said to him, "My father, if the prophet had told you to do some great thing, would you not have done it? How much more should you do it when he only tells you, "Wash and be clean?"*
>
> — 2 KINGS 5:13

Sometimes God purposes those around us to correct our thinking and help us realize the misalignments of our hearts. Naaman didn't miss the significance of their insights, and neither should we.

> *So Naaman went down and dipped himself in the Jordan seven times, according to the command of the man of God. Then his skin was restored and became like the skin of a small boy, and he was clean.*
>
> — 2 KINGS 5:14

God restored Naaman's physical body far beyond the mere healing of a skin disease. He made the skin of an old man like that of a young child. Don't miss this... God didn't just heal the disease, He actually transformed all of Naaman's skin into the vibrant, healthy skin of a toddler. Nothing transpired in the way Naaman expected or anticipated, and what a blessing that was.

> *Then Naaman and his whole company went back to the man of God, stood before him, and declared, "I know there's no God in the whole world except in Israel."*
>
> — 2 KINGS 5:15

God used Naaman's physical condition to transform his spiritual condition. God took Naaman's small bit of misguided faith and obedience to create a powerful testimony shared with his non-believing king, coworkers, friends, and family. Out of every negative, God will produce a positive.

We should never overlook the opportunities for obedience that God will place before us, and it is vitally important to follow God's instructions precisely as He commands, even when it doesn't make sense to us. I've pulled weeds in my garden at 5:30am in my pajamas because God said, "Go now". I've given far more financially to a friend in need, when I was struggling, because God said, "Give this now." I've stopped what I was doing to pray blessings over people who have hurt, rejected, and offended me because God said, "Pray this, right now."

None of it looked like what I thought it should. And from what I could see, none of it moved the needle in my season of waiting, either. But it was all planned and purposed by God to move the needle of my own faith; to align my heart under his authority; to remove pride and self-determination in me; and to prepare me for the answer to prayer before it arrived.

REFLECTION QUESTIONS:

1. Can you relate to Naaman? Is there a time when God gave you instructions, but you mentally processed it as unnecessary and never actually accomplished it?
2. What if the breakthrough you've been praying for doesn't arrive the way you've envisioned? Will you turn and walk away? What if it actually looks nothing like what you envisioned? Will you still be obedient to what God calls you to do?

_____

_____

_____

_____

_____

_____

_____

_____

_____

MY MARRIAGE WAS NOT BLESSED BY GOD, SO MAYBE I'M NOT SUPPOSED TO BE STANDING

DAY 32

The enemy will use every mental tactic in his arsenal to provoke questioning in your season of waiting including, "I never sought God's input on my choice to marry, so maybe God doesn't want me with them" Have you had a similar thought? Let's look at Joshua 9 and 10 to see God's response to a covenant entered into without his input or approval.

First, a bit of context: the people of Gibeon feared for their lives because Joshua and the Israelites were under God's favor and had well-known success in battle. That fear drove the Gibeonites to conjure up a deceptive story, a false truth, to seek a peace covenant with the Israelites. The leaders of Gibeon misrepresented who they were and where they were from to Joshua and the leadership. Joshua believed their lies. Scripture says,

> *But they did not seek the Lord's decision. Joshua established peace with them and made a treaty to*

> *let them live, and the leaders of the community swore an oath to them.*
>
> — JOSHUA 9:14-15

Three days later, the veil of deception was removed, and the truth was revealed. Today, we would render that covenant "null and void" because it was based on deception. A cancellation clause would give one party an exit strategy based on misrepresentation from the other party.

However, God's Kingdom does not operate as the world.

> *The Israelites did not attack {their covenant} people because they had sworn an oath to them by the Lord, the God of Israel.*
>
> — JOSHUA 9:18

The Israelites honored the very covenant they neglected to bring before the Lord for approval. Now, I can hear someone say, "Yeah, but I wasn't a Christian when I got married. I didn't enter that marital oath 'under the Lord'". Maybe not, but you're a Christ-follower now, and NOW is what matters. How you act **now**, what you choose **now**, is what matters.

How did Joshua react when their covenant relationship came under attack by an enemy?

> *Then the men of Gibeon sent word to Joshua in the camp at Gilgal: "Don't give up on your servants.*

> *Come quickly and save us! Help us, for all the Amorite kings living in the hill country have joined forces against us." So Joshua and all his troops, including all his best soldiers, came from Gilgal.*
>
> — JOSHUA 10:6-7

Don't miss this! Joshua and the Israelites defended the covenant. They defended those they were in a relationship with. Joshua didn't just give a half-hearted show of support; he appointed his best soldiers into the battle. They could have ignored the request, allowing the Gibeonites to be wiped out, and the covenant to expire. Joshua was obedient to the covenant, **even when the other party was at their weakest and unable to stand on their own.**

How did the Lord respond?

> *The Lord said to Joshua, "Do not be afraid of them, for I have handed them over to you. Not one of them will be able to stand against you." So Joshua caught them by surprise, after marching all night from Gilgal. The Lord threw them (the enemy) into confusion. As they fled Israel, the Lord threw large hailstones on them from the sky… and they died. More of them died from the hail than the Israelites killed with the sword.*
>
> — JOSHUA 10:8, 10-11

God honored their covenant. He honored the Israelites' obedience to the covenant, even though they were initially deceived, even when the Lord's approval was not sought, and even when a battle was before them. God will honor your commitment to stand for your marriage while He is orchestrating the outcomes. God will honor and bless your decision to stand and fight for your broken marriage, despite one of you being too weak, too deceived, or too faithless to fight for it.

Just like Joshua, we must show up for the battle, ready and armed with our prayers anchored upon scripture. Then we watch God do the actual fighting for us in the spiritual realm. Notice in the reported battle results that more of the enemy died by the God-produced hail storm than from mere humans holding on to swords. The spiritual realm did the fighting for them.

PRAYER PAUSE:

Lord Jesus, I lift the person reading this up to you in prayer. Thank you for the grace and mercy you give, even when we step ahead without consulting you. Thank you for honoring their covenant, even when it may not have been initially endorsed or established by you. Block every attempt by the enemy to discredit and discourage this person's obedient stand in faith. Holy Spirit, please impart wisdom and discernment into the hearts and minds of those standing for restoration, so that they may gain truth based upon your Word, not mine. Lord, I ask that your Living Water wash over those reading this and renew their stamina and strength to endure through the trials. Open their eyes to the truth you want them to understand, unique to their own situation. It's in Jesus' name, I pray. Amen.

WAITING WELL CHANGES EVERYTHING

WHAT AM I DOING WRONG? I DON'T UNDERSTAND WHY IT'S TAKING SO LONG FOR GOD TO MOVE.

DAY 33

You've prayed, fasted, anointed, and commanded "In Jesus' name" over the situation and yet nothing has worked. Now you're wondering what you're doing wrong and why there is no change in them or the situation. Is God even listening? Does He even care?

Assuming these acts in faith are done with a heart in right alignment with God, it's then important to realize you aren't doing anything wrong. Praying for a "distraction" (a person, work, vacation, money, materialism) to be removed in someone's life won't make their heart suddenly change. That distraction or idol in their life will always take priority because the distraction is not the actual root issue. The distraction is a symptom of a greater heart sickness and misalignment. You can pray a distraction out, but another will eventually fill the void. That empty space is only meant to be occupied by Jesus.

When Jonah was escaping from God's directive, he tried one distraction after another to avoid God's call on his heart. Yet God never stopped the pursuit because He was seeking a soul transformation for Jonah. God was patiently waiting for Jonah to surrender his own will for God's will.

While we wait, we fervently pray without ceasing for that person to step forward in repentance and commit to God ... not to us. Within the action of turning and repenting from a distraction, there is acknowledging and ceasing of a sinful behavior or breaking a soul tie, but these are all efforts that take a strength and conviction that only God can provide. Not us. There are no easy ways out of the muck and mire they get themselves into. It's a transformational process that guides their future decision making.

We, as prayer warriors, can stand firm on the sidelines, knowing God is orchestrating a glorious testimony. But we should accept that no amount of praying for a quick end or the removal of people and circumstances will bypass the hard work to be done. While we may watch God continually stir negative circumstances in someone's life to instigate a movement of their heart, it is still the person's decision to make. We are not puppets or robots. God seeks a relationship with us when we choose, not by His requirement. So that leaves us to either wallow in self-pity; demand some kind of relief from God; independently move on and go it our own way; OR... wait well and thrive in this season.

Choosing a relationship with God is a decision they make. Choosing the quality of the waiting season is a decision we make. I have chosen patience, and I have waited upon God's plan and purpose to unfold. I have pounded my proverbial stake in the ground and claimed this territory as mine to thrive within while I wait upon the Lord to move. There is much to do in God's Kingdom, and I am tremendously comforted and lean into the sweet words of God saying,

> *"... I will come and do for you all the good things I have promised, and I will bring you home again.*
>
> — JEREMIAH 29:10 NLT

I urge you to calm those fears that perpetuate you trying to control the situation, trying to always know what's going on in a prodigal's life. God knows far more than you, orchestrating details you can't even fathom nor consider. His ways are not our ways ... and thank God for THAT! Know that God has a specific purpose for what you see but don't understand. And also know that your prayers really are powerful and really do make a difference in God's Kingdom.

In this season, the Holy Spirit guided me to change my prayers to "God, please stir a deep and mighty discontent, dissatisfaction, and distaste in their heart for everything that is not YOUR best for them. Give them strength and conviction to step into the Holy Spirit's whisper, calling for their attention." It works!!! Notice that judgment over what is best in their life is left to God, not us.

Choose to stand in the gap and pray over them for true heart transformation rather than what you think will be the quickest trip to restoration. And then be courageous enough to pray for this stirring of the Holy Spirit in your own life. Seek God's direction to close doors and remove that which is not His best for your own life. Build faith in this season of what can feel like an exile; and know that your faith will always proceed the evidence that is most assuredly on the way.

> *Not one of all the Lord's good promises to Israel failed; every one was fulfilled.*
>
> — JOSHUA 21:45

REFLECTIVE QUESTION:

1. What would choosing patience look like in your situation? As God calls you to thrive in this exile, how can that look differently from where you are today?
2. Do you truly believe your prayers are powerful and make a difference? Ask God to give you the faith to believe that every prayer is heard and collected by Him. If you truly believed that how would your prayer life change?

PRAYER PAUSE:

Lord, it can be exhausting and frustrating to stand in the gap, but I know that is what you have called me to do. Please give me a fresh wind of patience and boldness for my prayer life. Stir in them a discontent, dissatisfaction, and distaste for everything that is not of you. And then do it in me. Transform my heart and build my faith. Electrify my prayer life and build confidence in me that every prayer I pray, no matter how small, is important to you. You don't call me to survive, You call me to thrive. Help me to walk in that calling. It's in your name, Jesus, that I pray. Amen."

CONSEQUENCES FOR "VENTING"

DAY 34

Moses was leading the Israelites out of slavery in Egypt to a promised land God had waiting just for them. As they neared the location, God instructed Moses to send a spy from each tribe into the new land, scout it out, and come back with a report of what they found. Keep in mind that this land was God's pre-ordained territory of restoration for His people. I'm thinking, would you really return with a report of anything except "Thank you and Amen"? Of course, that's not what happened.

All but two of the scouts returned with eyes and minds filled with fear, intimidation, anxiety, and negativity in their reports. Ten of the twelve scouts described what they saw through the filter of their fear rather than through the filter of faith and trust in ways the Lord had already provided. The people listened to the false news, the influencers of their day, and perpetuated the anxiety of those few. The people even threatened to stone those who gave a positive, encouraging report. Actually, it sounds a LOT like today.

> *All the Israelites complained about Moses and Aaron, and the whole community told them, 'If only we had died in the land of Egypt, or if only we had died in this wilderness! Why is the Lord bringing us into this land to die by the sword? Our wives and children will become plunder. Wouldn't it be better for us to go back to Egypt?' So they said to one another, "Let US appoint a leader and go back to Egypt." (emphasis added)*
>
> — NUMBERS 14:2-4

Don't miss the story's correlation and relevance to our own situations. The people thought they would be better suited to appoint a leader for themselves. They spewed words of negativity. They verbally vented their anxieties. They doubted God's provision, and because of it, they paid a massive price.

Society and the enemy have persuaded us to believe it is our right, and it is a mental health necessity to open the valve of pressure and release a hot mess of emotions. That's exactly what the Israelites did and here is how it went for them:

> *Then the Lord spoke to Moses and Aaron: How long must I endure this evil community that keeps complaining about me? I have heard the Israelites' complaints that they make against me. Tell them: As surely as I live–this is the Lord's declaration–I will do to you exactly as I heard you say. Your corpses will fall in this wilderness–*

because you have complained about me. I swear that none of you will enter the land I promised to settle you in... I will bring your children whom you said would become plunder into the land you rejected, and they will enjoy it... You will bear the consequences of your inequities for forty years based on the number of the forty days that you scouted the land, a year for each day. You will know my displeasure.

— EXODUS 14:26-35

While the Israelites eventually repented, and God was quick to forgive, He never removed the consequences of that behavior. The scouts who saw nothing but negative doom and gloom in God's provision *"were struck down by the Lord"*.

The enemy does a stellar job of deceiving us into thinking it's our right to vent and complain, that we deserve the opportunity to verbally process the details of what we see in front of us as "truth", but God's response has shown otherwise. Our words have the power to perpetuate the enemy's agenda to cast discouragement, despair, and darkness. Our words also have the power to speak life, to speak faith and trust, and to radiate Jesus, despite the circumstances.

I totally understand that this season of waiting on God is hard (trust me, I've been standing firm for many, many years), but you're not in this season without purpose. God is seeking to transform you. He will test your willingness...yes, willingness...to choose faith and trust, even when all you can see is a fog of fear and anxiety, in order to view the promise He has waiting for you. When He tests your yearnings and urges to vent and spew, it's your opportunity to deny those urges, focus your eyes and attention on the One who will overcome all the dysfunctions within your situation. Pray the blood and name of Jesus over all the details your flesh wants to condemn as impossible to change.

The Israelites failed to see God's provision. They paid the price for it. The entire generation of the older grumbling parents never placed a footprint onto the land God promised would flow with milk and honey. God commanded that all would die throughout the additional years of wandering in the wilderness. God's breakthrough and His blessing were reserved only for their children.

PRAYER PAUSE:

Lord, I pray that this urgency to share your message is planted deep within those reading and struggling ... Lord, when all that is in front of us seems so dysfunctional and unlikely to reach peace, joy, contentment, and glorious order, please convict us to move our vantage point off the details and onto you. We come to you in prayer, seeking relief from our pain, seeking clarity in the chaos, and seeking wisdom and discernment for our future steps. We need not circle the drain and spew emotions to everyone about everything that is not right in our situations. Lord, give us hearts of patience and endurance. Help us extend the same amount of grace and mercy to others as you give to us. Holy Spirit transforms us within and guide us through this difficult season. Help us to see that these stories within your Word are loving guardrails given to us by you to help us walk in victory. It is in your name, Jesus, that we pray. Amen.

WAITING WELL CHANGES EVERYTHING

PARTIAL OBEDIENCE IS STILL DISOBEDIENCE

DAY 35

Scripture doesn't say whether the Israelites spent their entire 40 years wandering the wilderness as a disgruntled and quarreling group. They started out the first two years complaining,

> *"Why did you ever bring us up from Egypt to kill us and our children and our livestock with thirst?"*
> *"Give us water to drink."*
>
> — EXODUS 17:2-3

And they ended the last year complaining,

> *Why have you brought the Lord's assembly into this wilderness for us and our livestock to die here? Why have you led us up from Egypt to bring us to this evil place? It's not a place of grain, figs,*

> *vines, and pomegranates, and there is no water to drink!*
>
> — NUMBERS 20:2-5

So it is likely that the middle wasn't much different.

During that early period, Moses cried out to the Lord,

> *"What should I do with these people? In a little while, they will stone me!" The Lord answered Moses, "Take the staff in your hand and hit the rock at Horeb; when you hit the rock, water will come out of it and the people will drink."*
>
> — EXODUS 17:4-5

Moses did exactly as he was instructed, and the Lord provided. Not only was this an opportunity to see God's glory and provision on display, but it was a leadership test for Moses to obey God's directives.

Forty years, many miles, and many miracles later, the Israelites demanded water again. They had grown tired of the manna miraculously appearing each morning, so God delivered quail. But the people still complained and wanted the variety of fruit and food they were accustomed to and missed back in the days of their slavery and bondage.

I can imagine Moses and Aaron were exasperated with all the complaining. As they sought guidance,

WAITING WELL CHANGES EVERYTHING

> *...the Lord spoke to Moses, "Take the staff and assemble the community. You and your brother Aaron are to speak to the rock while they watch, and it will yield its water. You will bring out water for them from the rock and provide drink for the community and their livestock.*
>
> — NUMBERS 20:7-8

Moses had been in the place of needing a miracle before. He had held the staff in his hand to obey God's directives frequently. But this time was different. Moses' actions were different. His words were different. And he paid dearly for that difference.

Scripture says,

> *Moses took the staff from the Lord's presence just as he had commanded him. Moses and Aaron summoned the assembly in front of the rock, and Moses said to them, "Listen, you rebels! Must we bring water out of this rock for you?" Then Moses raised his hand and struck the rock twice with his staff, so that abundant water gushed out and the community their livestock drank.*
>
> — NUMBERS 20:9-11

Moses! Moses!! What has happened to you? "Must WE bring water..."??? Don't you mean, must GOD bring water out of this rock? And what happened to following the directives? God said,

"*Speak* to the rock while they watch …" And yet, you hit the rock twice with your staff. Obedience is in the details. God certainly didn't overlook this partial obedience.

Maybe Moses was fed up with the complaining. Maybe he forgot and reverted to the instructions of the early years. Maybe he allowed his flesh and pride to steer the circumstances. His motivation was irrelevant; his actions were significant. Our lesson is imperative: Partial obedience is still disobedience to God.

Partial obedience may still gain the delivery of the miracle, just like water came from the rock and the people saw God's provision in overflow, but there are consequences to not following God's directives in the ways he commands. Moses and Aaron paid dearly for it.

> *"Because you did not trust me to demonstrate my holiness in the sight of the Israelites, you will not bring this assembly into the land I have given them," said the Lord.*
>
> — NUMBERS 20:12

We may think that was a harsh punishment after leading a group of disgruntled people around a wilderness for 40 years. We may look at the servanthood of Moses and Aaron and think they deserve more honor than simply viewing the land, but never allowed on the land. Actually, ALL the wandering, ungrateful, complaining elders died outside of the promise land. No one tasted the milk and honey promised all those years. That should scream volumes of how significantly important our willingness to follow directions means to God. Completing some of what God requests or accomplishing the request on our terms, in our ways, rather than his ways, is disobedience. Don't be lulled into thinking that God doesn't care how you get from point A to point B, as long as you eventually arrive at point B. It matters to God.

Learning to wait well upon the Lord means we are obedient and surrendered to the callings of God, in the ways that He requests. There will be many times when you think it shouldn't matter how you fulfill the request, but simply that you accomplished it. But the how matters.

Lord Jesus, I lift the person reading this right now and ask you to gently convict them of any outstanding tasks you've placed upon their lives. Give them a renewed urgency to complete what you've deemed as important, even if they do not see the importance. Please give them wisdom and discernment to walk in closer relationship with you. Lord, shower them with blessings with each completed assignment. Not that we do it for the blessing, but that you are such a wonderful Father to bestow your heavenly blessings despite our humanity and sinfulness. It's in your name, Jesus, that I pray, Amen.

REFLECTIVE QUESTIONS:

1. Has there been a previous time when you completed a task God gave you, but not in the manner that you knew it was to be accomplished? Did it change the way you viewed the outcome?
2. Is there an uncompleted task or assignment from God that is weighing heavily on your mind? Seek the Lord in

prayer for a renewed commitment to complete the task in the way He desires.

PRAYER FOCUS:

Lord, reveal to me any areas of my life in which I am walking in partial disobedience. I see now that even the little details are important to You. Thank you for being a God who doesn't miss a thing. Stir in me a sense of urgency to walk in full obedience to You and help me have spiritual eyes to see the assignments laid out before me. I can't walk in obedience without You, Lord, so I invite You in to help strengthen and guide me. It is in Your name, Jesus that I pray. Amen.

FOR YOUR CHILDREN'S CHILDREN...

DAY 36

One night during the pandemic lockdown, I was standing at the stove stirring a pot of boiling spaghetti and going through a list of work to-dos in my mind. Suddenly, this male voice spoke from behind me, "For your children's children." I stood frozen, perplexed, and repeating the four words over and over out loud. I knew the Holy Spirit had spoken, but understanding took a few minutes to gain. And then, swiftly, I felt the significance overwhelm me, bringing me to tears.

This season of standing is not for one singular purpose. Over time, I learned that standing was far more about the transformation of my heart for all of eternity, through the action of standing in the gap of faith for my spouse. What I had never stopped to realize is the generational impact of that obedience.

"For your children's children" is about seeing beyond our current situations and struggles to a future free of generational curses. Our kids and their kids are being restored back to Him in ways we could never comprehend before this walk started.

Fast forward two years, during the week before my first grandchild's birth, my four grown kids and their loves gathered to pray over the house and the nursery. Overwhelmed by the Holy Spirit's presence in that moment, I took several steps back from them to watch all that was before me. I listened to prayers of blessing, gratefulness, protection, provision, and faith spoken by each of these seven young adults, all now walking in relationships with God.

This passionate pursuit of God wasn't necessarily evident in any of us eight years ago. As a single parent, I was hardly the spiritual leader of our home. It wasn't until I got my heart right with God, when I started standing obediently and faithfully, and when I began walking out the plans and purposes of God in my life, that a radical shift happened in our home. The more I prayed and fasted over my children for the Holy Spirit to stir, the more God moved in significant ways. And now, on the eve of my oldest child having her first child, God reminds and reveals the full meaning of that night's revelation, "For your children's children."

Please hear me on this ... Your stand is NOT just about you reconnecting with your spouse. It's about breaking generational curses, some you know about, and others are dark family secrets buried in the past, roaming and wreaking havoc. It's about healing deep soul wounds that have been long buried and covertly festering within you. Standing is about obedience in the face of complete opposition to everything you see in front of you through faith and trust in the Lord. Faith and trust that HE will fight the battles necessary to bring about restoration and reconciliation for you, your children, and your children's children.

There were so many times on this journey that I wanted to give up. So many baits of the enemy urging me to "move on". And yet, through each manipulative act, I knew deep inside I was standing for something greater than me, even if I couldn't see it. Today, I see it. Four kids and their loves, all walking with the Lord. Generational prisons were busted open. Why? Because God is FAITHFUL to His children to restore their lives, their children's lives, and even their parent's lives.

Please understand that there is NOTHING special about me. I am a jacked up, sinful human who massively missed the mark repeatedly in my past life. But I am redeemed through Jesus. The prayers over my children were not, nor will they ever be, carried out in my strength or my prideful ways. It is only through continual repentance that I can kneel before a merciful God and seek the blessings over my family.

You have no idea how God will use your obedience; how God will honor your endurance, perseverance, trust, and faith in Him, despite the obstacles and hardships placed in your path. Don't look upon others in envy when they say they're done or moving on. Pray for them, because what they're moving away from could be the greatest movement of God they could never imagine. I'm living proof.

Every day I'm walking restoration out, even though there's little visual evidence to prove our marriage will be restored. Tears flowed that afternoon, listening to my kids pray over this little one about to be born. God allowed me to see behind the veil of how He was working in the lives of my loved ones, through prayer and fasting to Him, through my own actions of obedience and surrender to Him.

Please do not be deceived into thinking this journey is singularly about a short-term marriage on earth. This journey is changing lives, changing destinies for all eternity, and God wants you to play a significant role.

> *The Lord is slow to anger and abounding in faithful love, forgiving iniquity and rebellion. But he will not leave the guilty unpunished, bringing the consequences of the father's iniquity on the children to the third and fourth generation.*
>
> — NUMBERS 14:18 CSB

> *How happy is everyone who fears the Lord, who walks in his ways! You will surely eat what your hands have worked for. You will be happy, and it will go well for you. Your wife will be like a fruitful vine within your house, your children, like young olive trees around your table. In this very way, the man who fears the Lord will be blessed. May the Lord bless you from Zion, so that you will see the prosperity of Jerusalem all the days of your life and will see your children's children! Peace be with Israel.*
>
> — PSALMS 128:1-6

TAKE YOUR EYES OFF THE CIRCUMSTANCES. FOCUS ON ME

DAY 37

The Lord appeared to Abraham one day and spoke amazing promises over him, telling Abraham it was time to take a journey. God was going to make him into a great nation, create a legacy like none other, and use him to bless generations to come, all in a specially designated land. Genesis 12:1-9

The location was Canaan. The very place which God referenced, "I will give you this land." No confusion there. Abraham's feet were standing on this land at the very beginning of his journey. He and his tribe camped there. He built an altar to recognize God's promises and holy presence there. Note that God brought them directly to where He wanted them.

But then Abraham took his eyes off what God told him and placed his focus on a famine. Suddenly, the man building an altar and standing on holy ground allowed doubt, questioning and maybe even fear to enter his mind. What he saw around him spoke louder than God's voice of promise planted within him.

Can you hear the family and friends traveling with him?

"It's time to move on."

"God wouldn't want us starving here."

"Are you sure you heard God right?"

"Abraham, there's starvation all around us; how can we feed our families and livestock?"

"Maybe God didn't mean it for right now, but later ... when things don't look so impossible."

Abraham let his tribe of friends and family have greater voice in his decisions than what God had said directly to him. They all allowed the details they could see in the natural have more influence than what was spoken to them by God. Why do we allow the voices of others to cloud over the one voice we should stand firm upon? Instead of staying put, setting up residence and trusting God to provide all their needs in the famine, Abraham led his group onward. He kept moving instead of standing still.

> *If you don't stand firm in your faith, then you will not stand at all.*
>
> — ISAIAH 7:9

I have to wonder how many times God whispered, "Go Back", but the surrounding pressures were too distracting to hear it. Fear of the famine spoke louder than God's own voice. Abraham literally walked right into, through and out of the very place God said was his to possess. Has this happened to you in a relationship, job, friendship, or circumstance? How many times has God's promise or revelation been overshadowed and questioned by what you could see rather than trusting by faith?

I get it Abraham. I know your struggle. God has given me insight into what's coming that I never expected. But regardless, I need to stop, build an altar to honor Him, and then wait. Wait, even when others around me say it's time to move on. Wait, even when where I am standing is so far from what God has shown me. Wait, even when all that I see and hear says, impossible.

Wait.

> *For nothing will be impossible with God.*
>
> — LUKE 1:37

> *Wait for the Lord; be strong, and let your heart be courageous. Wait for the Lord.*
>
> — PSALMS 27:14

> *Now, if we hope for what we do not see, we eagerly wait for it with patience.*
>
> — ROMANS 8:25

REFLECTIVE QUESTION:

In what ways have you allowed what you see in front of you to speak louder into your heart than what God's Word says?

For each of those situations where what you see is vastly different from God's promise, I urge you to find a scripture verse to write over that past situation or current reality.

PRAYER PAUSE

Lord, forgive me for all the times that I, like Abraham, wandered from what you have said. Transform my heart and my mind to value what you have said over what others in my life have spoken. Open my spiritual eyes so that I may see my circumstances from a heavenly point of view, instead of the limited view I have that is defined by circumstances. Help me to stand firm in faith and trust you in the waiting. It is in your name, Jesus, that I pray. Amen.

_____
_____
_____
_____
_____
_____
_____
_____
_____
_____
_____

THE DAY AFTER BREAKTHROUGH

DAY 38

The door that has been shut for many, many years just opened up in what was to be a quick phone conversation. I called for one specific question, and upon expecting the call to end, I was surprised by hearing, "You don't have to hang up so quickly." Uhhh, okay?

He shared he had been experiencing an ongoing, radical encounter with God. His repenting was not a singular event but over days of anguishing soul convictions, which had left him depleted of his own strength, yet overwhelmed with God's love. He described reading the Bible with a new thirst and hunger not felt before and finding the Holy Spirit all too willing to meet him in his brokenness.

What surprised me most was that there was no surprise for me. Follow that? I was so confident in the eventual arrival of this moment that "suddenly" was never felt. God had been paving the way, brick by brick. Within this day after breakthrough, two of his phrases have been on repeat in my mind: "I never want to be out of the will of God ever again in my life" and "Thank you for never giving up on me." Overwhelmingly glorious.

During this day after breakthrough, the enemy has also been all too eager to minimize, spin doubt, and stir anxiety: "Did you really hear right?" "Are you making more out of it than actually happened?" "Don't get your hopes up." "You've heard this before, remember?"

I know the door to breakthrough has opened a few inches, just enough so that I can see beams of light streaming out. But this time I will not squeeze my fingers into the space to force open the door. I will not allow my own insecurities to have greater value and priority than his walk toward God. This WILL be different. Not because of the words spoken by Him, but because this time, my position and my authority under Jesus are securely anchored.

I choose to trust God. I choose to let the situation play out with no interference from me. I choose to marinate in the sweet words of "Thank you for never giving up on me" and "I love you," as he said goodnight during that phone call. In this long journey of years and years, I have learned that my relationship with God and his relationship with God are far more important than the short span of marriage and the restoration of it here on earth. What truly matters is the realignment of his heart under God's authority, and his desire to never be out of the will of God again.

Please hear this! I never would have been blessed to hear those beautiful sentiments if I had listened to the enemy's relentless message to stop standing, or if I tried to fill the void with someone else. These many years have been hard for sure, but those years have been my boot camp, building perseverance and endurance in me; strengthening my trust, faith, and hope in the Lord, and preparing me for a different battle about to be waged. Those years have transformed me to be the woman, wife, and mother God originally designed me to be, according to His will, plan, and purpose for my life.

It's important for me to pause here and tell you, the reader, that the above writing, The Day after Breakthrough, was experienced and journaled two years ago. While everything in the spiritual realm shifted that day, nothing in the natural realm looks any different two years later than it did the day before the phone call happened. In these silent moments, when I do not know what is going on, I'm choosing to stand firm in the promise God gave to both of us years ago. I'm choosing to give God all the glory and honor in these moments.

God, you've blessed me with the gifts of patience, contentment, and joy in the midst of waiting. You've taught me what waiting well means, and I know this time is about your healing and repentance within him. Lord, I lift him up to you. Please give him the strength, wisdom, and discernment to keep walking towards you. Meet him deeply and permanently on his journey.

I am forever anchored by God's love, grace, and mercy. I am content and willing to wait upon the Lord. I will share my testimony, support and serve others in this walk. For God never wastes a single moment of our hardships, and for this I lift my hands in praise.

> *Let us hold tightly without wavering to the hope we affirm, for God can be trusted to keep his promise.*
>
> — HEBREWS 10:23

REFLECTIVE QUESTIONS:

1. Have you experienced a breakthrough moment(s) in your stand? As you reflect upon it, how can that experience strengthen your faith, even if it did not exactly come to pass in the way you planned or imagined?
2. As you look at this standing season as your own bootcamp, what lessons have resulted? What has the Holy Spirit shown you? What testimonies can you reap from the tests God has allowed in your life?

_____

_____

_____

_____

_____

_____

_____

WAITING WELL CHANGES EVERYTHING

BACK TO THE BEGINNING

DAY 39

The Holy Spirit just reminded me of a visiting pastor's sermon at our church. I urgently go to my closet, pull out boxes of journals filled with years of writings, and search for the details spoken by him in July 2019. Pastor Andreas Nielsen stated that a Chinese bamboo tree needs to be watered daily for five years. In that long period of watering, you can't see any progress, no growth at all. You just keep watering and watering every day for five years. During the fifth year, a little green sprout pushes out of the ground. Five weeks later, the tree explodes in size to about 90 feet. Think about that ... we only witness the last five weeks of rapid growth in a long five-year commitment to its daily waterings.

Pastor Nielsen continued,

> *Christ says we're like a seed planted in the soil. Has God put something in your heart that is so big you don't even have friends you can tell it to? Maybe it's so big it scares you. Maybe it's so far ahead and*

you feel like you've been doing this for so long and yet you still can't see it. Friends start questioning you. They don't understand that we don't live in a five-week mentality. We live in a God-mentality where the five years of nothing is sometimes what it takes to get five weeks of success. God can break ground in your life at any time. Remember, the size of the harvest is in direct proportion to how much you sow."

Pray, Pay and Stay, July 2019. Riverbank Church.

Today, time apart and distance have built even greater mountains and detachment between that promise and me. Is it possible that God has been watering that seed and promise every day for the last five years, anticipating a little sprout to break through the ground? Is it possible that 90 feet of a promise can rapidly grow in five weeks?

This journey of restoration rests only in the Master Gardener's hands. It is not mine to know, but only to water by prayer. I move forward in life with eyes focused on God. My obedience is to Him alone. My life is surrendered to His will. God has allowed me to navigate massive highs and sinking lows, joyful moments, and heartbreaking pain to encourage growth, trust, faith, endurance, love, joy, peace, and patience through Him.

Go figure ... During all this time of standing, during all these days where I was faithfully watering a seed of relational restoration with my prayers, the Master Gardener had also planted a seed in me, to harvest the fruits of the Spirit, with His Living Water fortifying me daily.

WAITING WELL CHANGES EVERYTHING

For the word of the Lord is right and true; he is faithful in all he does.

— PSALMS 33:4

Wait! Ohhh my goodness!!! Is it possible? Could I actually be the Chinese Bamboo tree? Could the one God has been quietly and silently watering day after day for the last five years be me? Could I be the one who has experienced the breakthrough and the tremendous growth?

This journey. The heartache. The rejection. The pain. Trading pride for humility. Swapping independence for faith. ALL OF IT. Every day, every hour was allowed, appointed, and ordained by God, to bring about His purpose and His calling in my life, to prepare me for His eternity, and then to transform me into the woman, wife, and mother He always intended for me to be.

This means that God owned every moment! He truly collected every tear. He had a purpose for ALL OF IT. With every person God placed in my path, I have heard His prompting, "Tell them. Show them what I've shown you." Could this book you hold in your hands be the growing evidence of a seed planted five years ago and watered faithfully every day?

Please hear me Friends, for you truly are my brothers and sisters on this standing journey, for all these days, months, and maybe even years, that you may have been hyper focused on the reconciliation of your marriage, on the return of your prodigal, on the completion of a promise requested in prayer, please, please don't miss the awareness that God has been orchestrating His most important reconciliation first ... the one between you and Him. Stand confidently from there, knowing all else will follow.

> *Now, if anyone is enfolded into Jesus, he has become an entirely new person. All that is related to the old order has vanished. Behold, everything is fresh and new. And God has made all things new, and reconciled us to Himself, and given us the ministry of reconciling others to God. We are ambassadors of the Anointed One who carry the message of Christ to the world, as though God were tenderly pleading with them directly through our lips. So we tenderly plead with you on Christ's behalf, "turn back to God and be reconciled to Him."*
>
> — 2 CORINTHIANS 5:17-18, 20

> *Remain in the things which you have learned and have been assured of, knowing from whom you have learned them.*
>
> — 2 TIMOTHY 3:14

_____

_____

_____

_____

WAITING WELL CHANGES EVERYTHING

FORTY DAYS

DAY 40

When I first felt the pull from God to write this devotional, I didn't understand why He was specifically leading me to 40 days. Why not 14 or 21, or even 30 days?

Out of obedience, I gathered my writings and assembled them as I felt His leading. I knew that, while the individual topics held purposes for learning, it was the collective ordering that exemplified how waiting well over time truly could change a life. While preparing a focus group to review the days of material, the Holy Spirit prompted me to rearrange the latter days of writings, remove two, combine two others, and add two new devotions, which left Day 40 today without an entry. I spent Sabbath Saturday in quiet reflection, anticipating the Holy Spirit's arrival with words of great wisdom that I would simply dictate.

Then God reminded me of His question during the pandemic lockdown: "Kelly, I've given you the end of the story. Are you going to trust me with how we get there?" And so, God began showing me a recap of seven times when the Bible referenced a 40-day journey.

In Genesis 6 and 7, God sought Noah's assistance in His plan to create an earthly reset from sin. With specific dimensions and use of materials, Noah followed the construction plans engineered by God to build a boat. "I will make it rain on earth for 40 days and nights," God said. "Everything on earth will perish. But I will establish my covenant with you and you will enter the ark ..." God gave Noah the end of the story but required obedience and trust.

In Exodus 24 through 34, Moses was summoned to the top of Mount Sinai, fasting and abiding in God's presence for 40 days, while God downloaded His commandments, laws and instructions to His servant. God gave Moses the end of their restoration story and required trust from the Israelites and their leader to get there.

In Numbers 13 and 14, God instructed twelve men to play the role of spies, to scour and survey the Promised Land and return with a report. After 40 days, ten of the men returned scared and discouraged, reporting what they saw through the filter of their fears and insecurities. Only two men, Caleb and Joshua, reported their experiences through the glorious provisions of their Heavenly Father. God gave the Israelites a promised land and sought their obedience, faith, and trust to step upon it.

In 1 Kings 19, Jezebel threatened the life of Elijah and he became afraid. It took two visits from an angel of the Lord, providing nourishment and support for Elijah to walk out the 40 days. God gave Elijah the provisions and plan, seeking His trust and obedience to see it through.

In 1 Samuel 17, Goliath taunted the Israelites day after day. When the Israelites heard the verbal threats and challenges from this Philistine, they retreated. After 40 days of continual retreat, a teenage shepherd boy named David leaned into God's supernatural strength and defeated an enemy that loomed far larger than the Israelites' faith. God gave David the end of the story, and David trusted the Lord in how to get there.

In Jonah 3, after disobediently fleeing from God and ending up in a horrible place, Jonah followed God's instructions and went to Nineveh. Once in the city, he declared to its citizens, "In 40 days, Nineveh will be demolished!" God gave Jonah a prophecy for the end of the story, but Jonah's own prideful judgement got in the way. Meanwhile, it only took one day for Jonah to declare the message of destruction for Nineveh's people, and their hearts turned back to God. When they were presented with the end of their story, they trusted God in His plan and purpose to redeem.

And, in Matthew 4, the Holy Spirit led Jesus into the wilderness for a 40-day preparation to be encountered by the enemy. Jesus knew the end of the story. He, HIMSELF, was the story, and He was acutely aware of the ending. But through it, He modeled for us trust and faith in His Father right to the very moment when He exhaled, "It is finished."

Within each one of these seven stories, 40 days were purposed by God to fulfill a plan for transformation. Noah, Moses, Caleb, Joshua, David, Elijah, Jonah, and, even Jesus, had to walk out 40 days of preparation in one season to prepare for the next season. And the same can be said for our walks with the Lord.

The enemy's darkness was all throughout these seven stories, casting, stirring, and weaving doubt, discouragement, and fear. This same presence is seeking dominance and influence within our lives today. But God has given us the end of our stories. His Word never lies, and it never runs dry of the Living Water that will sustain us in this long season.

My stand during these seven years, my spiritual growth in these five years, and our time together in these 40 days equates to more than what I could ever see on the surface with my eyes. And the same is true for you. As you stand in the gap of faith between your loved one and God, it is your BOLD prayers that become the physical bridge upon which a holy restoration has been ordained.

God has given us all the tools we need. He has already orchestrated the end of our stories. He only asks of us, *"Will you trust me with how we get there?"*

WAITING WELL CHANGES EVERYTHING

WALKING OUT OF THE WILDERNESS...LESSONS LEARNED OF LOVE AND MARRIAGE IN A SEASON OF WAITING

DAY 41

Thought our time together was done? Ha! So did I ... As you read yesterday, this devotional was intended to be 40 days in length. But then the Holy Spirit reminded me that when Jesus exited the wilderness on day 40, He did so with lessons, insights, and strength gained during His season of pressing and testing. Day 41 was about walking out of the wilderness in God's plan and purpose, prepared and informed. So what have been your lessons learned on this journey? Here are some of mine:

1. We aren't supposed to be fighting for a person's love, affection, time, and attention. Our sole focus should be to become the man or woman God has uniquely designed each of us to be. We are not to place our efforts on trying to convince the other person of God's calling over their lives or the viability of the promise. God doesn't need our help. This includes begging for their quick return to the home, convincing them of how we've changed, or using God to force and manipulate that which we seek.

When you place all your attention on becoming who God calls *you* to be, your reflection of Jesus permeates every aspect of your life. God can then open the heart of the one you love to see Jesus within you. The joy, peace, and contentment (all the fruits of the Spirit) are blessings others see within you and desire for themselves. This happens only because you've cleared out the mind and heart interferences, and God can work on you and your spouse. Even if the other person is a nonbeliever, God can use you to transform a hardened heart. But that can't happen when you are focused on "fighting" for someone or seeking the return of what used to be. Be a window through which they can see Jesus and watch what can happen!

2. Take your eyes off the other person and focus squarely on God. In the story of Peter walking on water, he said, "Lord, if it's you, command me to come to you on the water." Jesus said, "Come." Peter then climbed out of the boat and started walking on the water. But when he saw the strength of the wind, he was afraid, and beginning to sink he cried out, "Lord, save me!" Matthew 14:28-30.

How many times have we called out to God, but then taken our eyes off God and started looking at the chaos and storms around us? We look at the social media posts. We analyze what someone is doing or not doing, saying or not saying. We judge the other person based on what our eyes see within the storm rather than intently focusing on Jesus, as He's called us, to walk on top of the raging seas.

3. A Godly marriage is not an end-all goal. I used to look at other marriages around me and think; I want THAT. Like I could hit the heavenly "Buy Now" button and gain it without putting in the time and effort. Abiding in a Godly marriage is a transformational journey that occurs when each spouse has their own right-standing with God. It is the resulting fruit produced on a healthy tree. Each person chases hard after God and supports the other person's walk with the Lord. Jesus becomes the Superglue between them, as their blessed marriage becomes a daily journey rather than a single destination to be arrived at.

4. A marital relationship with God is like a triangle. God is the top point of the triangle and you and your spouse are the bottom two points. As each of you walks toward the top point of the triangle, you get closer to God, but also move closer to each other. Sometimes one spouse may be further along in that journey than the other, but that's okay. Just keep walking it out in faith. Maintaining the same spiritual pace and where the other may be in their walk is not the focus. Concentrate on Jesus, confident that He has everything else under His control.

5. Prayers really DO matter. Pray for the salvations of your spouse, ex, estranged or not. Pray for Godly men and women to be placed in their path, to speak into and influence their walks. Pray for the Godly realignment of relationships in the life of that "other person" who may be part of the circumstances. Pray in the authority given to you, in Jesus' name, to bind up and cast out evil spirits and fill that void only with the Holy Spirit. Pray for wisdom and discernment for yourself. And above all, repent, repent, and then repent again ... keep your vessel clean of bitterness and all things not of God. He needs a clean vessel to pour into. And then, power pack those prayers with specific scripture verses. Anchor yourself upon the Word. Bold prayers WILL move mountains when God's Word is incorporated into our communications and made a part of our daily lives.

6. God redeems time. We get so hyper focused on counting the days, months, and years that may pass in this season of waiting. We hope for the next holiday to be different. We want the next family reunion to be "the one" that testifies to God's redemption and restoration. But limitations of time for us are irrelevant to God. Repeatedly, I've read testimonies about how God moved in mere days and weeks to achieve results that people thought would take years. We perceive and assume the timeframes for transformations based upon our own understandings. We place conditions upon returns and expectations for what reconciliation should look like that are not God-glorifying. We can't comprehend how a multi-year breakdown of a relationship can be reorganized in a matter of days or weeks ... BUT GOD!

7. And finally, God loved us so much that He willingly gave His Son to shoulder the penalties of our jacked-up mistakes. I urge you not to read this and move on, but soak in it. From the first days of creation, God orchestrated His Son to stand in the courtrooms of our lives and receive the rightful punishments due to us. God is far more concerned with the condition of our hearts because our relationships with God secure our eternity. The Bible is a perfectly orchestrated, redemptive plan to reconcile and restore us to Him. If God went through all this effort to re-establish us in right-standing with Him, then we can trust and stand in His promises coming to pass in our lives. We can trust that all things really are possible for God.

Your things ... my things ... all things.

WAITING WELL CHANGES EVERYTHING

> *I am certain that I will see the Lord's goodness in the land of the living. Wait for the Lord; be strong, and let your heart be courageous. Wait for the Lord.*
>
> — PSALMS 27:13-14 CSB

If you have walked these 40 days and now stand at your own Y in the road, you're not alone, spiritually or literally. Going to the left direction means a life as you've been living. Years of an independent, self-determined, I know what's best for me, kind of walking produces a suitcase busting at the seams with the emotional results of that walk, surrounded with the same people going in the same direction. Even complete chaos and dysfunction in life can become a comfort zone when you've lived in it long enough.

As you ponder what the days will look like after today, know that Jesus is found on the narrow path to the right, ready to walk with you on that journey. When we acknowledge His rightful place as Lord and Savior, when we seek forgiveness and cleansing of our past through repentance, and when we step willingly into a relationship with Jesus, life from this day forward will never be the same. Consider this prayer ...

> *Jesus, I come to you at the end of myself, at the end of my prideful choices, my judgements, and self-determinations. I leave the wreckage of my life at the foot of your cross, where you willingly gave your life so that I could live a life in freedom, not just for tomorrow but for all eternity. Jesus, you are my Lord and Savior. I seek to obediently walk in your plan and purpose for my life. Grant me wisdom and discern-*

ment to guide my days and be a source of help for others who are coming behind me on a similar journey. Open my eyes to your truths in scripture, as they build confidence in me that your promises will come to pass. While I abide in you, show me the true and abundant significance of what being a child of your Heavenly Father truly means. Bless my new walk, as I give glory to you and testify of all you have done and will do. In Jesus' name and the power of His blood and resurrection, I pray this over my life. Amen.

> *Even now–this is the Lord's declaration - turn to me with all your heart, with fasting, weeping and mourning.*
>
> — JOEL 2:12

> *Turn to me and be saved, all the ends of the earth. For I am God, and there is no other.*
>
> — ISAIAH 45:22

This is the message of faith that we proclaim: If you confess with your mouth, "Jesus is Lord," and believe in your heart that God raised Him from the dead, you will be saved. One believes with the heart, resulting in righteousness, and one confesses with the mouth, resulting in salvation. For the scripture says,

> *Everyone who believes on Him will not be put to shame, since there is no distinction between Jew and Greek, because the same Lord of all richly*

blesses all who call on Him. For everyone who calls on the name of the Lord will be saved.

— ROMANS 10:9-13

As we walk the days towards the fruition of our promises, please never forget Waiting Well Changes Everything.

—Kelly Murphy

WAITING WELL CHANGES EVERYTHING

STAND ANCHORED ON THE PROMISES

What are the promises from God? To begin unpacking that I decided to do a quick search on YouTube and found multiple meditative videos titled God's Promises. While the scenery and background music were soothing, I quickly realized that these content creators were often mixing scriptures describing human actions, responses and emotions with actual promises made by God to us, His children.

For example, in Joshua 24:15,

> *But as for me and my house, we will serve the Lord.*

That is not a promise from God. It's a beautiful declaration of human obedience and steadfastness to serve the Lord, but it's spoken by a human, who like all of us, has a sin-nature.

If I'm going to be anchored during a massive storm blowing through my marriage, my health, or the lives of my children, I want that anchor to be deeply lodged into a rock that never shifts, never cracks, nor dissolves. Eternal permanence is what I am seeking.

I greatly encourage you to delve into the chapter and book from which each of these verses originate in the Bible. Understand the context – people, place, history – that underpins why the scripture is a promise from God; what was happening for God to extend his grace and mercy. For example: everyone loves to state Jeremiah 29:11 ... "For I know the plans..." But did you know this verse was spoken to God's chosen people while they were in slavery? God was reassuring them in a time of tremendous bondage and exile. Content matters.

> *God is not a man, that He should lie, nor a son of a man, that He should repent. Has He said, and will He not do? Or has He spoken, and will He not make it good?*
>
> — NUMBER 23:19

> *For all the promises of God in Him are Yes, and in Him Amen, to the glory of God through us.*
>
> — 2 CORINTHIANS 1:20

> *Therefore, whoever hears these sayings of Mine, and does them, I will liken him to a wise man who built his house on the rock. And the rain descended, the floods came, and the winds below*

and beat on that house; and it did not fall, for it was founded on the rock.

— MATTHEW 7:24-25

Do not remember the past events; pay no attention to things of old. Look I am about to do something new; even now it is coming. Do you not see it? Indeed, I will make a way in the wilderness, rivers in the desert.

— ISAIAH 43:19 CSB

But I will bring you health and will heal you of your wounds – this is the Lord's declaration.

— JEREMIAH 30:17

The angel of the Lord encamps around those who fear him and rescues them. Taste and see that the Lord is good. How happy is the person who takes refuge in him!

— PSALMS 34:7-8

Now this is what the Lord says – the one who created you, Jacob, and the one who formed you Israel – "Do not fear, for I have redeemed you; I have called you by your name; you are mine. When you pass through the waters, I will be with you, and the rivers will not overwhelm you. When you walk through the fire, you will not be scorched, and the flame will not burn you. For I am the Lord your God, the Holy One of Israel, and your Savior."

— ISAIAH 43:1-2

The Lord is near the brokenhearted; he saves those crushed in spirit.

— PSALMS 34:18

Do not fear, for I am with you; do not be afraid, for I am your God. I will strengthen you; I will help you; I will hold on to you with my righteous right hand. For I am the Lord your God, who holds your right hand, who says to you, "Do not fear, I will help you."

— ISAIAH 41:10,13

I will instruct you and show you the way to go; with my eye on you, I will give counsel.

— PSALMS 32:8

The Lord will always lead you, satisfy you in a parched land, and strengthen your bone. You will be like a watered garden and like a spring whose water never runs dry.

— ISAIAH 58:11

The Lord is the one who will go before you. He will be with you; he will not leave you or abandon you. Do not be afraid or discouraged.

— DEUTERONOMY 31:8

Because he has his heart set on me, I will deliver him; I will protect him because he knows my name. When he calls out to me, I will answer him. I will be with him in trouble. I will rescue him and give him honor. I will satisfy him with a long life and show him my salvation.

— PSALMS 91:14-16

"No weapon formed against you will succeed, and you will refute any accusation raised again you in court. This is the heritage of the Lord's servants, and their vindication is from me." This is the Lord's declaration.

— ISAIAH 54:17

Jesus said to him, "'If you can?' Everything is possible for the one who believes."

— MARK 9:23

Looking at them, Jesus said, "With man it is impossible, but not with God, because all things are possible with God."

— MARK 10:27

Jesus replied to them, "Have faith in God. Truly I tell you, if anyone says to this mountain, 'Be lifted up and thrown into the sea,' and does not doubt in his heart, but believes that what he says will happen, it will be done for him. Therefore, I tell you, everything you pray and ask for – believe that you have received it and it will be yours. And whenever you stand praying, if you have anything against anyone, forgive him, so that your father in heaven will also forgive you your wrongdoing."

— MARK 11:23, 24

For the Lord God is a sun and shield. The Lord grants favor and honor; he does not withhold the good from those who live with integrity. Happy is the person who trusts in you, Lord of Armies!

— PSALMS 84:11

No temptation has come upon you except what is common to humanity. But God is faithful; he will not allow you to be tempted beyond what you are able, but with the temptation he will also provide the way out so that you may be able to bear it.

— 1 CORINTHIANS 10:13

Keep your life free from the love of money. Be satisfied with what you have, for himself has said, I will never leave you or abandon you.

— HEBREWS 13:5

"Come to me, all of you who are weary and burdened, and I will give you rest. Take my yoke upon you and learn from me, because I am lowly and humble in heart, and you will find rest for your souls. For my yoke is easy and my burden is light."

— MATTHEW 11:28-30

"For I know the plans I have for you" – this is the Lord's declaration – "plans for your well-being, not for disaster, to give you a future and a hope. You will call to me and come and pray to me, and I will listen to you. You will seek me and find me when you search for me with all your heart. I will be found by you."

— JEREMIAH 29:11-13

He gives strength to the faint and strengthens the powerless. Those who trust in the Lord will renew their strength; they will soar on wings like eagles; they will run and not become weary, they will walk and not faint.

— ISAIAH 40:29, 31

The Lord is good to those who wait for him, to the person who seeks him.

— LAMENTATIONS 3:25

For God loved the world in this way: He gave his one and only Son, so that everyone who believes in him will not perish but have eternal life. For God did not send his Son into the world to condemn the world, but to save the world through him.

— JOHN 3:16-17

"See! I stand at the door and knock. If anyone hears my voice and opens the door, I will come in to him and eat with him, and he with me."

— REVELATION 3:20

...the word of the Lord came to Jeremiah a second time: "The Lord who made the earth, the Lord who forms it to establish it, the Lord is his name, says this: Call to me and I will answer you and tell you great and incomprehensible things you do not know."

— JEREMIAH 33:3

"Ask, and it will be given to you. Seek, and you will find. Knock, and the door will be opened to you. For everyone who asks receives, and the one who seeks finds, and to the one who knocks, the door will be opened."

— MATTHEW 7:7-8, 11

Serve the Lord your God, and he will bless your bread and your water. I will remove illnesses from you.

— EXODUS 23:25

He heals the brokenhearted and bandages their wounds.

— PSALMS 147:3

The Lord is near the brokenhearted; he saves those crushed in spirit. One who is righteous has many adversities, but the Lord rescues him from them all.

— PSALMS 34:19

The Lord will sustain him on his sickbed; you will heal him on the bed where he lies.

— PSALMS 41:3

But the Counselor, the Holy Spirit, whom the Father will send in my name, will teach you all things and remind you of everything I have told you. Peace, I leave with you. My peace I give to you. I do not give to you as the world gives. Don't let your heart be troubled or fearful.

— JOHN 14:26

For nothing will be impossible with God.

— LUKE 1:37

For the Scripture says, Everyone who believes on him will not be put to shame, since there is no distinction between Jew and Greek, because the same Lord of all richly blesses all who call on him. For everyone who calls on the name of the Lord will be saved.

— ROMANS 10:11-13

"For truly I tell you, if you have faith the size of a mustard seed, you will tell this mountain, 'Move from here to there,' and it will move. Nothing will be impossible for you."

— MATTHEW 17:20

Jesus answered them, "Truly I tell you, if you have faith and do not doubt, you will not only do what was done to the fig tree, but even if you tell this mountain, 'Be lifted up and thrown into the sea,' it will be done. And if you believe, you will receive whatever you ask for in prayer."

— MATTHEW 21:22

STAND ANCHORED ON THE PROMISES

> *Call on me in a day of trouble; I will rescue you, and you will honor me.*
>
> — PSALMS 50:15

> *But Moses said to the people, "Don't be afraid. Stand firm and see the Lord's salvation that he will accomplish for you today; for the Egyptians you see today, you will never see again. The Lord will fight for you, and you must be quiet."*
>
> — EXODUS 14:14

SCRIPTURES & NOTATIONS DAY BY DAY

Introduction
Joel 2:12
Isaiah 45:22

Day 1
John 11:5-6
John 11:11
John 11:4
2 Peter 3:9

Day 2
Matthew 11:28-30
Deuteronomy 4:36
James 1:5-6

Day 3
Psalms 119 CSB

John 8:32
Proverbs 2:7 TPT
John 5:24 NLT
Psalms 91:4
Hebrews 4:12
Ephesians 6:10-13

Day 4
Matthew 19:6
Hebrews 4:12 CLB
Psalms 145:18 CSB

Day 5
Psalms 62:1-2

Day 6
Zechariah 6:8

Day 7
Psalms 147:3
Psalms 34:18
Proverbs 18:10

Day 8
Romans 5:3-5 NLT

Day 9
1 Kings 13:18
1 Kings 13:22

Day 10
Psalms 39:7
Romans 15:13
Hebrews 11:1
Romans 5:5
Hebrews 6:19
Jeremiah 29:11

Day 11
Exodus 14:11-12
Exodus 14:1-2
Isaiah 43: 1-2, 5

Day 12
Mark 16:14 CSB
James 1:6
Mark 11:23
Romans 4:20
Matthew 19:26

Day 13
Deuteronomy 8:2
Deuteronomy 8:3
Deuteronomy 8:6-7, 9
Deuteronomy 8:17
Deuteronomy 9:6
Deuteronomy 11:8
Deuteronomy 11:12

SCRIPTURES & NOTATIONS DAY BY DAY

Day 14
Jeremiah 29:11
Jeremiah 29:5-6
Jeremiah 29:7
Jeremiah 29:8-9

Day 15
Isaiah 7:9

Day 16
Jeremiah 31:21
Jeremiah 33:3

Day 17
Investopedia definition of "red flag"

Day 18
Ephesians 6:12
James 1:6
Isaiah 7:9
Hebrews 11:6

Day 19
Luke 1:45
Psalms 27:14

Day 20
Mark 9:29 KJV, CSB, NIV, NLT, & ESV
Jonah 3:5, 3:10 ESV
Acts 13:2

Isaiah 58:6
John 6:35 TPT
John 4:14 TPT

Day 21
2 Chronicles 3-4
2 Chronicles 15-17
Acts 16:25

Day 22
Genesis 16:2
Genesis 16:5
Genesis 21:1-2
Genesis 21:7
Jeremiah 32:27
Mark 11:23

Day 23
Job 1:7-8
Job 1:9-12

Day 24
Daniel 6:10
Daniel 6:17
Daniel 6:19-27
Luke 10:19 KJV

Day 25
Jonah 1:16

SCRIPTURES & NOTATIONS DAY BY DAY

Day 26
Jonah 1

Day 27
Romans 5:3-5

Day 28
Matthew 12:38-39
Matthew 16:4

Day 29
Luke 4:18-19 CSB
Matthew 12:43-45
Luke 11: 24-26

Day 30
Matthew 6:14
Luke 23:34

Day 31
2 Kings 5:10
2 Kings 5:11-12
2 Kings 5:13
2 Kings 5:14
2 Kings 5:15

Day 32
Joshua 9:14-15
Joshua 9:18
Joshua 10:6-7

Joshua 10:8, 10-11

Day 33
Jeremiah 29:10 NLT
Joshua 21:45

Day 34
Numbers 14:2-4
Exodus 14:26-35

Day 35
Numbers 20:2-5
Exodus 17:3,2
Exodus 17:4-5
Numbers 20:7-8
Numbers 20:9-11
Numbers 20:12

Day 36
Numbers 14:18 CSB
Psalms 128:1-6

Day 37
Isaiah 7:9
Luke 1:37
Psalms 27:14
Romans 8:25

Day 38
Hebrews 10:23

SCRIPTURES & NOTATIONS DAY BY DAY

Day 39
"Pray, Pay, and Stay." Voices Series Part 2. Riverbank Church, Guest Pastor Andreas Nielsen; 21:07
Psalms 33:4
2 Corinthians 5:17-18, 20
2 Timothy 3:14

Day 40
Genesis 7
Jonah 3
Matthew 4

Day 41
Matthew 14:28-30
Psalms 27 CSB

ABOUT THE AUTHOR

Kelly Murphy is an author, a consultant, and, most importantly, a woman who values faith, family, and making a positive impact on the world. When she's not guiding readers on their journeys of faith through her inspirational books, she's lending her expertise to non-profit organizations as a dedicated consultant.

- facebook.com/waitingwell.today
- x.com/waitingwell2day
- instagram.com/waitingwellchangeseverything

www.waitingwell.org

ABOUT THE PUBLISHER

"Everyone has a story to tell, only the courageous will find a way to get it told. Let my team and I help you become courageous!"

Helping people become courageous is something we have been doing since LakeView Publications was founded in 2018.

How Do I Get My Book Published?

Finding the right publisher is key. The team at LakeView Publications is driven by our passion to help people tell their stories and in helping them find a way to allow their story to take them to the next level.

You reach out to us with the best way to reach you, and we do the rest. It's that easy!

You wrote the book; we do everything else!

www.LakeviewPublishers.com

facebook.com/LakeviewPublishing

instagram.com/lakeview_publishing

Want to Publish Your Book?

We Can Help!

* Manuscript Editing

* Book Cover

* Book Formatting

*Illustrations

* Publishing through all major retailers (Amazon, Kobo, B&N, Apple)

* Paperbacks & eBooks

* Blurb Writing

* Audio Books

* Choose Your Own Package

* Author Retains **ALL** rights

We're here to help!

"Everyone has a story to tell, only the courageous will find a way to get it told. Let my team and I help you become courageous!"

LAKEVIEW
PUBLICATIONS

www.LakeviewPublishers.com

Made in United States
North Haven, CT
24 October 2024